JOHN A. MACDONALD
The Man and the Politician

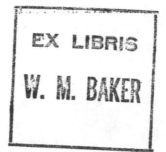

JOHN A. MACDONALD

The Man and the Politician

Donald Swainson

Toronto

OXFORD UNIVERSITY PRESS

1971

ISBN 0–19–540181–6

© Oxford University Press (Canadian Branch) 1971

2 3 4 5 6 – 6 5 4 3 2 1

Printed in Canada by
John Deyell Limited

Contents

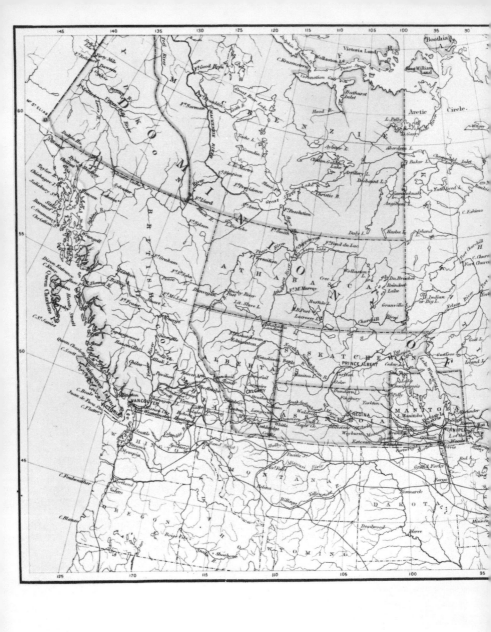

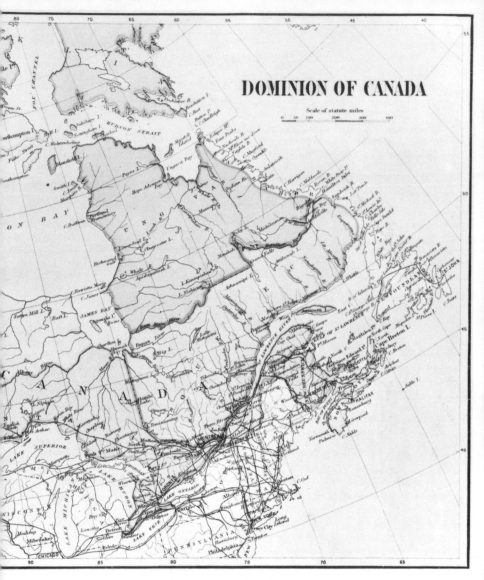

Macdonald's Canada: the 1890s

Illustrations

Except where otherwise mentioned, all illustrations are
reproduced by courtesy of the Public Archives of Canada

Preface

Sir John A. Macdonald (1815-91), the most famous of all Canadian leaders, was an attractive and complex human being. He was endowed not only with high intelligence, but with charm and wit. He enjoyed convivial company and had an irresistible sense of humour, which he was capable of turning upon himself. He was a man of passion and temper, a plotter and a heavy drinker. Though his personal life was filled with tragedy and loneliness, he was very sensitive to the feelings of others. This quality helped to make him one of the two or three greatest political managers in our history. "When this man is gone," Goldwin Smith wrote in *The Week* in 1884, "who will there be to take his place? What shepherd is there who knows the sheep or whose voice the sheep know?"

Macdonald's impressive skills as a politician were used for more than narrow and partisan purposes. During the mid-1850s he attained a position of dominance that he never lost. The politics of that decade were petty and local. But beginning in 1864 things changed and Canadian leaders were involved in an impressive series of creative acts and terrifying adventures: confederation; the Red River Resistance; the extension of Canada from sea to sea; the Pacific Scandal; the depression of the 1870s; the construction of the CPR; provincial rights agitations; the North West Rebellion of 1885.

Macdonald was closely involved in all these events, which confirmed his belief in strong leadership. "My experience", he once commented to a friend, "has been that when the directing mind is removed, things always go wrong." For a generation Macdonald was Canada's directing mind and it is therefore impossible to understand the man without studying these great events of nineteenth-century Canada.

Macdonald's career was unusually long, perhaps because of his great flexibility and persistent optimism. He sat in Parliament for forty-seven years and his cabinet experience stretched over forty-four. He was elected at various times for five different constituencies and during his career held seven cabinet posts as well as the prime ministership. At the time of his death in 1891, Sir Wilfrid Laurier correctly said that Macdonald had "one of the most remarkable careers of this century".

Macdonald was not above utilizing corruption, but this fact pales beside his achievement as a nation-builder and consolidator dedicated to a free and tolerant Canada. "We should accept as men and brothers," he once said, "all those who think alike of the future of the country, and wish to act alike for the good of the country, no matter what their antecedents may have been." He not only helped to create Canada but contributed immeasurably to its character.

Note

In order to avoid confusion, the use of certain terms must be explained. "British North America" refers to all of Britain's North American possessions. These territories form Canada as it is today. Between 1791 and 1841 the present provinces of Ontario and Quebec were separate colonies called Upper Canada (Ontario) and Lower Canada (Quebec). They were united into a single colony in 1841 called the "Province of Canada"; it was usually referred to simply as "the Union". Its two sections were re-named "Canada West" (Ontario) and "Canada East" (Quebec). At confederation in 1867 they became the central provinces of Ontario and Quebec in the Dominion of Canada, which included Nova Scotia and New Brunswick and eventually the other Maritime colonies, Prince Edward Island and Newfoundland. Rupert's Land was the vast northern territory controlled by the Hudson's Bay Company until 1870 when the area was annexed by Canada; it included parts of northern Ontario and Quebec, and most of what is now Manitoba, Saskatchewan, and Alberta.

1

Origins of a Statesman

Hugh Macdonald, John A.'s father, was an ambitious man. When he grew up he moved from Dornoch, Scotland, where he was born, to Glasgow in order to be a success in business. There he entered into a partnership to manufacture cotton. He married Helen Shaw, an intelligent Highlander, and they had five children. Their first, William, died in infancy. Margaret was followed a year and a half later by John Alexander, who was born in Glasgow on January 11, 1815. He had a younger brother, James, and a baby sister called Louisa.

Though Hugh was ambitious, he was also easygoing, fond of liquor, and a poor businessman. The manufacturing business failed, and so did a second venture. Times were bad and success in Scotland seemed beyond his reach. He thought of emigrating. Upper Canada could provide a fresh start, for Helen Macdonald had relatives in Kingston, the "King's Town".

In the summer of 1820 Helen and Hugh and their four young children made the long, miserable Atlantic crossing. After landing at Quebec they travelled up the St Lawrence to Montreal, then on to Kingston by *batteau*, an inelegant flat-bottomed craft that advanced under a combination of sail and pole and sometimes oxen, which were used to pull the boat through especially dangerous waters. The journey from Quebec City to Kingston lasted three weeks. When they arrived there in July the Macdonalds went directly to the home of Lieutenant-Colonel Donald Macpherson, whose wife was a half-sister to Mrs Macdonald. Hugh and his family were made welcome.

John Alexander Macdonald was five years old when his family arrived in Kingston. (He would be intimately associated with the town and surrounding district for seventy-one years.) Kingston had fewer than 4,000 citizens in 1820, but despite its small size it was a major town, superseded only by Toronto, the capital of Upper Canada. Situated at the junction of Lake Ontario and the great St Lawrence River, it was both a naval and commercial centre, the acknowledged Loyalist capital, and the chief town of the Midland District, which included four counties. It was old for Upper Canada, with a history dating back to the seventeenth century, and it was charming. Its grey limestone walls and buildings clustered near a waterfront that overlooked a serene view of green islands and sparkling waters. In Macdonald's day all parts of the bustling town were close to Lake Ontario or the Cataraqui River.

Hugh was confident that Kingston was the place for him. Opportunities appeared to be plentiful. Shortly after his arrival he opened a small general store, and the living quarters above became the family's first Canadian home. But once more prosperity passed Hugh Macdonald by: he failed again. The Kingston venture was further marred by the death of little James. Years later a relative described the tragedy: "His father and mother were going out for a walk in the evening, and the little fellow ran after them asking to be allowed to accompany them. It was thought better not to take him, and he was sent back to the house under the care of the servant-man. The latter was one of those rough beings who have no sympathy with the woes of children, and, when the child did not cease crying, gave him a push or a blow, and he fell on an andiron with such force that he was fatally injured and died in a few days."

In 1824 Hugh moved his family a few miles west to Hay Bay, a lush green farming community on the Bay of Quinté. Another shop was opened and yet another failure was quickly recorded. Harassed and disillusioned, the Mac-donalds then tried Prince Edward County, a rich triangular peninsula that juts into Lake Ontario forty miles west of Kingston. There, at Glenora on Adolphus Reach, Hugh Macdonald bought a mill. This venture could hardly be called a success, but neither was it a failure. For several years the family eked out a barely adequate living and was happy. Though not very interested in sports, John was an outdoor boy who became a fast runner and in winter liked to skate. He and his sisters hiked and played and explored the local countryside. John loved to play soldier. He was always the leader while Moll and Lou (as his sisters were called) were troops under his command. They fished in the mysterious Lake-on-the-Mountain, which is perched on a plateau hun-dreds of feet above the waters of Adolphus Reach. Its attrac-tions were enhanced by a legend that said the lake was fed by an underground tunnel that connected it with Lake Erie! In any event the fish were neither legendary nor mysterious. Lake-on-the-Mountain abounded in pike, pickerel, perch, and bass.

Education is generally important to Scottish people and was so to the Macdonalds. Despite family poverty and very limited opportunities, John received what training was avail-able. When he was about seven he began primary school in

Kingston but was obliged to leave when his family moved. During their brief stay at Hay Bay, John and his sisters had attended school three miles away at Adolphustown, a long walk for children. There was no school at Glenora, so John, who was nine in 1824, was sent back to Kingston. He boarded with friends and attended first the Midland District Grammar School and in 1829 a new Presbyterian school. (At least two of his schoolmates there, John Hillyard Cameron and Oliver Mowat, later became important political leaders.) Then his formal education, limited but sound, ended when Hugh and Helen Macdonald decided that John should become a lawyer.

Upper Canada had no law school in 1830. If a young man wished to study the law he became a lawyer's apprentice and learned the profession through on-the-job training. Such young men were called "articled students". In 1830 John was articled to a young but important Kingston lawyer, George Mackenzie. As was the custom, John boarded with his master, and the fifteen-year-old boy began an entirely new life. No longer could he spend long afternoons loafing with school friends, nor could he devote his summers to fishing and playing with Moll and Lou at his father's mill. Instead he was required to go each morning to Mackenzie's law office, where he acted as a messenger, clerk, and stenographer. He toiled in the office by day and in the evenings studied law under the supervision of George Mackenzie. Years later Macdonald commented, "I had no boyhood. From the age of fifteen I began to earn my own living."

John possessed an excellent intelligence, a love of reading, and an industrious nature. It quickly became clear that he was a responsible lad and had a natural aptitude for the law. His studies progressed rapidly and Mackenzie was suitably impressed. George Mackenzie was an ambitious lawyer. In 1832 he opened a second office at Napanee, a few miles west of Kingston, where Macdonald was appointed manager. Napanee was just a sleepy little village, and important cases could be referred to the boss in Kingston. Nonetheless Macdonald was given considerable independence when he was only seventeen. He appreciated this sign of recognition, enjoying both the work and the responsibility.

In Kingston the Macdonalds had many relatives and friends, but in Napanee John was on his own in every respect. He found it easy to make friends with Donald Stuart and Thomas Ramsay. These close chums enjoyed each others' company and spent hours discussing the problems of the day and indulging in horseplay. Macdonald, who had a lifelong appetite for books, read widely in history, law, literature, and biography, and he remembered much of what he read.

1833 was an exciting year. When George Mackenzie had to leave Kingston for several weeks, John was recalled to take charge of his office—a considerable honour for a young man of eighteen. Later in the year another opportunity presented itself. John had a cousin, Lowther Pennington Macpherson, who was the lawyer at Hallowell in Prince Edward County. At this time he was a sick man who needed a long rest without any professional responsibilities, and he asked Macdonald to take over his practice until he recovered. John agreed and, still a teenager, took over a general practice. Technically he was still a student who could not be admitted to the bar until he was twenty-one, but at Hallowell he was completely on his own. He did well. His stay was the more pleasant because it brought him back to his family who still operated the mill at Glenora, only a few miles from his office. Once again he could spend time with Moll and Lou and his parents. In the next year, when he was nineteen, he held his first political office as Secretary of the Prince Edward District School Board. Opportunities were plentiful for able young men.

Hallowell was pleasant, but John wanted more than the little village could offer. He wanted to be a man of affairs, and that meant going back to Kingston, which was the commercial, military, political, and social centre of the Midland District.

Macdonald's door of opportunity was opened by a tragedy. In 1834 Upper Canada was devastated by a cholera epidemic. Kingston was not spared that dreadful visitation; almost 300 Kingstonians died during the grim summer months. One of them was Macdonald's old mentor and teacher, George Mackenzie, whose death raised an important question. Who would fill his role as the leading lawyer within Kingston's Scottish Presbyterian community? Mackenzie's professional successor would automatically become a man of influence and wealth. Still in his teens, Macdonald was determined to qualify for that position. He returned to Kingston in 1835 to open his own law office on Wellington Street. A year later he was finally admitted to the bar of Upper Canada as a full-fledged lawyer. He was now a qualified professional, ready and anxious to put his mark on the world.

At the age of twenty-one Macdonald was in charge of his own law firm. His understanding of the law was shrewd and intuitive; even more important, he had an almost unnerving ability to understand the strengths and weaknesses of others, which stood him in good stead during his long and often frenetic career. No sooner had he been admitted to the bar than he expanded his office by acquiring two law students of his own. Oliver Mowat came immediately. When he was followed a couple of years later by Alexander Campbell, the little office contained an extraordinary threesome: a future Prime Minister of Canada, a future premier of Ontario, and a future Lieutenant-Governor of Ontario.

In 1836 Hugh Macdonald's mill failed and he returned to Kingston to become a bank clerk. For John's easy-going, indolent father it was the end of the road. He was forced to admit even to himself that he was too lax and weak to function as an independent businessman. The strongest member of the family was now John, and for the remainder of his life he was the real leader of the Macdonalds.

He was almost six feet tall and slender, with a mass of long dark curly hair that covered part of his coat collar and flopped over his ears. His chin was strong, his forehead high, and his nose so large that it became a standing joke. Macdonald loved stylish clothes and was a striking-looking man, but he was not handsome. In fact he was famed for his homeliness. Once when his sister Lou was told that she closely resembled John A., she replied angrily, "A curious compliment to pay to me, considering that John Macdonald is one of the ugliest men in Canada." Macdonald himself had no illusions about his looks. When he commented on the condition of a somewhat tired old horse, its owner replied, "Faith, he's like yourself, sir, a bit worse for wear." Macdonald replied, "Yes, he's like myself, a rum 'un to look at, but a rare 'un to go."

Easy of manner and with a superb sense of humour, Macdonald made new friends with ease and his friendships were permanent ones. His fondness for company led him to join a host of organizations: St Andrews Presbyterian Church, the Young Men's Society, the Orange Order, the

Masons, and the St Andrews Society, the ethnic organization for Kingston's Scots. This was a special interest and Macdonald became a leading member.

Macdonald's friends, professional associates, and relatives were almost without exception Conservatives. Like most of his fellow townsmen he breathed deeply of Kingston's Tory air and became a Conservative. But he was the sort of Conservative who could be flexible and realistic. Facts were always facts to him and could not be brushed aside by political ideology. He lived in a world of real men and real problems. Conservatism was his guide, not his straitjacket.

Professional success came easily to this attractive young man with his instinctive friendliness and extensive knowledge of the law. Within a few years he was recognized as a first-class and courageous courtroom lawyer. As far as Macdonald was concerned all accused men, regardless of their unpopularity, deserved a defence. In 1837 he defended a bitterly hated child raper. His client was hanged, but Macdonald gave him the best available defence and Kingstonians admired his courage. After the Rebellion of 1837 and the unprovoked raids from United States territory in 1838, Macdonald was involved in several important cases. He successfully defended eight men accused of treason. He also gave legal advice to a group of raiders from American territory. Led by Nils von Schoultz, these Americans confronted Canadian and British troops at Windmill Point, east of Prescott. Sixty Canadians were wounded, sixteen were killed, and a young Canadian lieutenant suffered mutilation. Needless to say, bitterness was rife and Macdonald risked his popularity in advising the Americans, who were tried by court martial. They had no real defence and the leaders faced sure execution, but Macdonald did what he could. Again he displayed his courage and showed that he was a moderate Conservative, not a hidebound reactionary. By 1838 Macdonald's position was secure. He was a public figure, a popular young man, and a senior lawyer.

2

A Life's Work

The tragic Rebellion of 1837 convinced the British authorities of the need for a new Canadian constitution. Lord Durham was made Governor-General, charged with the task of investigating the ills of Upper and Lower Canada. Within a remarkably short time Durham completed his famous *Report*. His chief recommendation was that Upper and Lower Canada be fused into one colony. The British authorities accepted this advice and by the Act of Union created the Province of Canada. The new colony was to have a single parliament in which Canada West and Canada East were to have an equal number of members. The official life of the Province of Canada began in 1841.

The new constitution revolutionized Canadian politics. But more important for John A. Macdonald, Kingston became the capital of a huge colony extending from Gaspé in the east to Lake Superior in the west. He knew that important decisions, crucial struggles, and dramatic events would take place before his eyes. As his political appetite was whetted, he became more active within the Conservative Party.

Politics might be attractive, but Macdonald was not yet ready for a public career. He was only twenty-six in 1841, and other problems occupied most of his attention. His law practice needed cultivation and already Macdonald was indulging in the common nineteenth-century custom of combining law with business. In 1839 he was elected a director of the Commercial Bank of the Midland District. Later in the same year he was appointed the bank's lawyer. This was an important and profitable account, which provided Macdonald with a substantial portion of his income. Other important clients were quickly acquired.

During this phase of his career he was often ill. The exact nature of his disease is unknown, but in 1840 and 1841 he was laid up from time to time. In September 1841 he was doubtless depressed by his father's premature death, which added to his family responsibilities. Politics still beckoned, but there was no time.

Macdonald knew that without his health he would be unable to enjoy a successful career. In order to recover fully after his 1841 illness he decided to take a long rest in Britain. An interesting incident preceded his departure. John A. was fond of liquor, but he was not usually a gambling man. Nonetheless he indulged in a three-day game of loo shortly before going abroad. Loo is a vicious card game of high risk, involving heavy losses and equally impressive winnings. Aided by a long lucky streak, Macdonald won a great deal of money in that mammoth gambling session and headed for Britain, in January 1842, with his pockets full of other men's pounds, shillings, and pence.

His holiday in Britain was carefree and happy and his health quickly improved. He saw the sights of London, Windsor, Oxford, and Cambridge, purchased a good-sized law library and some house furnishings in London, and travelled to Scotland to see relatives. Macdonald's entire life was altered by this visit, for he met a pretty cousin named Isabella Clark. We have no way of knowing what passed between them, but it must have been pleasant for "Isa" resolved to visit her Kingston relatives in the following year.

Fully recovered from his mysterious illness, rested, and filled with optimism, Macdonald returned to his neglected law practice in the summer. He was happy to be back at work. While still abroad he explained to his mother: "To a person obliged during all his life to be busy, idleness is no pleasure and I feel assured I shall return to my desk with greater zest and zeal than ever."

In 1843 Macdonald finally plunged into active politics. He made a successful bid for a seat on Kingston's City Council and on March 28 became Alderman John A. Macdonald.

Isabella's arrival in the summer was the other important event of the year. The young people fell in love and almost immediately decided to marry. After a rapid courtship and a short engagement they were married on September 1. They were doubtless social lions in the Kingston of 1843. John A. was a dashing young alderman and a successful lawyer. Isabella was a charming if somewhat gushy woman, described years later by Macdonald's cousin, James Pennington Macpherson, as having a "sweet gentleness of manner and tender sympathetic nature". "Their house", according to James Macpherson, who visited it as a small boy, "was large and commodious and contained all the comforts and conveniences then known to Canadian civilization. There was also a fine carriage and a pair of horses, 'Mohawk' and 'Charlie'." The Macdonalds were obviously fond of the devoted little James and assured him that he could visit as often as he liked. The boy felt very much at home with the Macdonalds. "Here I spent some of the happiest days of my life, being allowed the honour of sitting beside the coachman if the carriage was

John A. Macdonald, 1842

taken out, or at other times, the almost equally enjoyable privilege of being my uncle's companion in his library. We seldom talked: he was deep in his books, while I had a corner to myself where were gathered together . . . numerous illustrated books and such captivating tales as *King Arthur and His Knights of the Round Table, The Arabian Nights Entertainment,* etc., etc. I have no doubt but that I was often troublesome, but I cannot recollect ever receiving from him one unkind word."

The young Macdonalds were warm people with a happy domestic life. They enjoyed the companionship of numerous relatives and close friends. Domestic bliss, however, rarely overcomes political ambition. John Macdonald was determined to play a part in the larger drama of Canadian public life. Within weeks of his marriage, he was given a chance to display his political skills.

In November 1843 Parliament agreed to transfer the capital away from Kingston, which Robert Baldwin once dismissed with contempt as an "Orange Hole" because the city was a stronghold of the staunchly Conservative Orange Order. When Montreal was selected for the honour, Kingstonians were enraged. Macdonald helped to direct the powerful protest movement that resulted. He knew there must be an election soon and his ambition was to become Kingston's M.P. Close association with this local movement gained him much public support and he was well prepared for the 1844 election. Two hundred and twenty-five of his fellow citizens petitioned Macdonald to run. He agreed and campaigned furiously.

The campaign witnessed the usual violence and heavy drinking. Voters expected candidates to supply them with large quantities of whisky, which sold for 25c a gallon.

Macdonald obliged and crushed his poor opponent by winning 275 to 42. It was a glorious personal victory, for throughout the province the Conservatives managed to win only a narrow majority of a few seats. Macdonald's triumph confirmed his popularity. In November 1844 he was off to Montreal to attend his first session of Parliament. Alexander Campbell, once his law student but now his partner, agreed to run the law office during his absence.

Politics were very unstable and confused during the 1840s. A careful analysis of that situation cannot be included here, but Macdonald's role must be sketched briefly if his career is to be understood. When Macdonald went to Montreal in 1844, a Conservative régime under the leadership of William Henry Draper held power, but just barely. It could not survive without the strong backing of the Governor-General, Sir Charles Metcalfe. "Sweet William" Draper was in serious political trouble. His cabinet was threatened from two directions. The external danger was the Liberal opposition led by Robert Baldwin and Louis LaFontaine. Their position was so strong that they might destroy the government at almost any moment. Internally the danger was division and dissent. Draper's party was torn by conflict between moderate Conservatives, of which Draper himself was one, and old-fashioned Family Compact Tories like Sir Allan MacNab and his more moderate ally, Macdonald's onetime schoolmate John Hillyard Cameron. This bitter division was not finally resolved until the middle of the 1850s. It was important to Macdonald because, like other Conservatives, he could not avoid involvement in the struggle for the soul of his party. About his position there could be no doubt: he was an unwavering supporter of Draper and the moderates.

As a freshman M.P., Macdonald cut an interesting figure.

"His face", explained a nineteenth-century student of his
career, "was smoothly shaved, as it always was, and he had
the appearance of an actor. His walk then, as ever after, was
peculiar. His step was short, and when he went to a seat,
there was something in his movement which suggested a bird
alighting in a hesitating way from a flight. His quick and
all-comprehending glance, and that peculiar jerking of the
head, bore out the comparison in other respects." Macdonald
was discreet and made no attempt to outshine his seniors.
Never an orator, he actively disliked much of the bombastic
speech-making of the period. He was essentially a debater,
and he quickly became expert in the use of the quick retort
and the piercing question. Shortly after his arrival in Montreal, Macdonald was acknowledged as an expert on parliamentary rules and election law. He was making a name for
himself, but he was doing it slowly and methodically.

Macdonald had no alternative but to act slowly because he
was soon engulfed by family tragedy. It began in 1844 when
Isa took ill. Her health returned but the illness was a serious
one and it recurred the following year. She never recovered;
for the remainder of her life she was an invalid, wracked by
pain and in constant danger of death. Often quantities of
opium were required to make her existence bearable. Nurses
and doctors were in constant attendance and domestic bliss
gave way to perpetual horror.

Young Mrs Macdonald was so ill during the summer of
1845 that John all but gave up hope for her recovery. He
explained the mysterious ailment to her sister: "She is
weaker than she has ever yet been, and there are symptoms,
such as an apparent numbness of one limb, and an irregular-
ity in the action of the heart, that made me send for Dr
Sampson, although against Isabella's wish. He saw her this

morning and says he cannot relieve her, and I ought not, my beloved sister, to disguise from you that he thinks her in the most precarious state. I would not write thus plainly to you, did I not know your strength of mind, and the impropriety of concealing anything from you. I do not therefore hesitate to tell you, that unless God in his infinite mercy works an immediate change for the better, it is impossible for her to remain in her exhausted state for many days." John was convinced that his wife needed better medical care than was available in Kingston and a period of rest in a warm climate. Movement was dangerous but he took the fearful chance. Isa was taken across Lake Ontario to the American side. "The exhaustion produced by carrying Isabella down to the boat", wrote her terrified husband, "was dreadful to witness. We thought she would die on the deck. We had risked everything, however, on the chance, and though sorely tempted to return, we remained on board." John took Isabella to New Haven, then to Savannah, Georgia. The trip, though long and exhausting, improved Isa's health a bit and Macdonald was able to return to Canada early in 1846 after an absence of six months. Isabella had to remain in the United States for three years.

Macdonald's professional, family, constituency, and parliamentary responsibilities produced intolerable pressures. From time to time throughout his life he would break away—retreat from familiar scenes, sometimes alone, sometimes with a friend, and drink heavily. During this period, for example—the exact date is not known—Macdonald and another young lawyer, John Rose of Montreal, made a strange visit to the United States. Years later Lord Carnarvon described the incident: "Macdonald . . . told a curious anecdote of his early life. When quite a young man he and Sir John Rose, and a third, whose name I forget, went into the States and wandered about as strolling musicians. Macdonald played some rude instrument, Rose enacted the part of a bear and danced, and the third did something else. To the great amusement of themselves and everyone else, they collected pence by their performance in wayside taverns, etc." The player of the "rude instrument" was a Conservative member of Parliament!

A caustic tongue and a vicious temper were other aspects of Macdonald's character. In the spring of 1846 he made a slurring remark about the Boulton family of Toronto in the hearing of William Henry Boulton, M.P. for Toronto. The Boultons were powerful Compact Tories and William Henry was an important politician. So bitter was Boulton's reaction that the two men almost fought a duel. During a passionate debate a few years later Macdonald was infuriated by a long partisan harangue of William Hume Blake, one of the leaders of the Liberal party. Macdonald's detestation of the rich, haughty Irishman ran so deep that he challenged him to a duel, which was prevented by the Assembly's Sergeant-at-Arms. Nobody could accuse John A. Macdonald of being a cold-blooded man.

During these years of "great struggle for power and place", as Macdonald once defined politics, his career advanced. In 1846 he was appointed a Queen's Counsel, and in 1847 Draper offered him the junior post of Solicitor-General. Macdonald refused, perhaps because of financial problems or possibly because of Isabella's chronic illness. She was in New York, where John had gone for Christmas, and now her illness was seriously complicated. Isabella was pregnant. She was delighted and in all probability so was Macdonald. Nonetheless he was a desperately worried man. In August 1847 Isabella gave birth to John Alexander Jr, almost losing her life in the process. They loved the little boy despite the circumstances of his birth and the perils that threatened his mother.

In the meantime Macdonald had been persuaded to enter the cabinet. In May 1847, when he was thirty-two, he became Receiver-General. So strong was his position within the Conservative Party that he could start thinking about real leadership. It would not be easy, but with work and skill he could become Draper's successor as leader of the Conservatives of Canada West. Eminence and power brought headaches as well as satisfaction. While there was little time for his law practice, his bills remained heavy and his debts became heavier. As a key cabinet minister he was required to spend huge amounts of time in Montreal. With Isabella chronically ill, relatives were obliged to care for his infant son. Macdonald was lonesome, worried, and overworked.

Personal pressures were increased by political problems. The Conservative government was dissolving. "Sweet William" Draper, determined to quit politics, finally resigned office in May 1847 to become a judge. Perhaps even more serious was the onset of a depression that produced unrest and discontent throughout the land. Knowing that it was finished, the badly buffeted government decided to go down with a burst of grandeur. It held an election in December 1847-January 1848. Macdonald's easy win in Kingston was exceptional: throughout the province Conservatives went down to defeat. They resigned office in March 1848, to be replaced by the great Liberal government led by Robert Baldwin and Louis Hippolyte LaFontaine.

The Conservative defeat on this occasion came at an opportune time. Isabella returned to Kingston in June 1848 and John was able to spend time with her while she was reunited

"Bellevue", a Macdonald home in Kingston, Ont.

with her little boy. Three years in the States had produced no cure and Isabella remained an invalid. That was the central fact of Macdonald's domestic life. Even the baby found it difficult to adjust to a chronically ill mother who had been absent for so long. "At first", explained Macdonald, "he was shy and uncomfortable in her room, which is in some degree darkened, and as she could not dandle him, or toss him about, a ceremony which the young gentleman insists upon from all who approach him. He is now however great friends with her, and sits most contentedly in the bed with her surrounded by his toys."

Isabella needed rest and solitude so Macdonald rented a large house in the country west of Kingston. Bellevue, which is now a delightful museum, had "a fresh breeze ever blowing on it from Lake Ontario" and was "completely surrounded with trees." It had been built by a grocer with social pretensions. Large, awkward, and ornate, it tickled Macdonald's funny-bone. "I have taken a cottage or rather, I beg its pardon a *Villa*. . . . It is a large roomy house. . . . The House was built for a retired grocer, who was resolved to have a 'Eyetalian Willar', and has built the most fantastic concern imaginable. From the previous laudable tho' rather prosaic pursuits of the worthy landlord the house is variously known in Kingston as Tea Caddy Castle, Molasses Hall and Muscovada Cottage." Macdonald favoured the name "Pekoe Pagoda", but agreed that "it is not respectable either for a man or a house to have an alias." An "appropriate name" was needed and "Bellevue" was the name selected. Macdonald was reminded of a riddle by the profession of Bellevue's original owner. "Why", he asked, "is mixing wine or adulterating sugar a more heinous crime than murder?" To the groans of his audience he replied, "Because murder is a gross offence but adulterating sugar is a *grocer* offence."

Once settled into their new house, the Macdonalds picked up the threads of their disrupted family life. Isabella did her best. "Poor soul," reported Macdonald to his sister-in-law, "you will wonder to see her management of household affairs from her bed. She is like the 'Invisible Lady' that used to exhibit not 'show' herself some years ago. The invisible Lady's voice, orders and behests are heard and obeyed all over the house, and are carried out as to the cupboards which she never sees and pots and pans that have no acquaintance with her. Not a glass is broken or set of dishes diminished, but she knows of, and calls the criminal to account for." This pleasant change from the separation and chaos of the three preceding years could not last. On September 21, 1848 baby John suddenly died. Gloom descended once more upon Macdonald's household.

Politics provided no pleasant distraction from these family horrors. From Macdonald's point of view the political scene could hardly have been worse. The Liberals, with a sweeping majority, had established the new constitutional principle of Responsible Government. With strong French-Canadian support they carried out extensive reforms. Many Conservatives, especially Tories of the old school, were depressed and bitter about the new régime. They regarded LaFontaine and his French-Canadian followers as disloyal men with no right to govern. Their mood became blacker and uglier until they made fools of themselves by going to wild and stupid excesses. The final straw was the signing by Governor-General Elgin of the Rebellion Losses Bill, designed to compensate those who suffered financial loss during the 1837 rebellion in Lower Canada. To the Tories this was not compensation for loss but reward for treason. They lost their heads and resorted to mob violence. Lord Elgin was humiliated and jeered by mobs incited by Tory demagogues. His very life was endangered when "he was assailed with stones, clubs, and rotten and good eggs by thousands." The Parliament Buildings in Montreal were burned, with the loss of Canada's 20,000-volume parliamentary library. Furthermore, many leading Conservatives announced their support for the annexation of Canada to the United States! For years these men had worn their loyalty like a party button. When the going got rough, however, they threw aside their traditions and beliefs, abused the representative of Queen Victoria, and announced their willingness to end the existence of Canada as a separate country. They quickly came to their senses, but for years the Conservatives were taunted about their 1849 binge.

Mercifully Macdonald was not involved in his party's disgrace. Ultra-Tories, not moderate Conservatives, were the real culprits. In any event Macdonald was at home in Kingston much of the time. He quickly dissociated himself from the extremist elements in his party by helping to organize the British North American League. It condemned both violence and annexation, recommending instead constructive policies like protective tariffs for Canadian products and the confederation of British North America.

Montreal's mob frightened the politicians. Wanting no repeat performance, they decided to move the capital. This was the origin of the famous "seat-of-government question", for it proved almost impossible to select a capital city satisfactory to most Canadians. Initially the capital alternated between Toronto and Quebec City. Everybody agreed that this cumbrous and expensive system could not last. For years Kingston, Toronto, Montreal, Bytown (now Ottawa), and

Quebec City fought for the honour. Another divisive issue
had been injected into the already complex politics of the
Province of Canada.

In 1851 political fluidity returned when LaFontaine and
Baldwin retired from public life. A new Liberal government
headed by Francis Hincks and A. N. Morin was formed and
was confirmed at a general election held late in 1851. Although the Conservatives did poorly, Macdonald emerged
from the election with his prestige greatly enhanced. Along
with his usual easy win in Kingston he presided over a
Conservative sweep in the Midland District.

Sir Allan Napier MacNab, a bilious, gouty old Tory, was
the official leader of the Canada-West Conservatives. But
after 1851 there was little doubt about Macdonald's position.
He was the brains of the party and its effective parliamentary
leader—the real director, in fact, of the Conservative Party.
None of his associates could seriously challenge his position.
Nothing was more important to the Conservative Party than
Macdonald's rise to power for it meant a transformed Conservative policy on the question of French Canada. Unlike the
ultra-Tories, John A. did not regard French Canadians as
traitors who should never rule. Like Draper he regarded them
as the logical partners of the Canada-West Conservatives. His
plan was to form an alliance with French Canadians: they
would become full partners within the Conservative Party
and the country. He explained to Brown Chamberlain, a
Montreal newspaperman: "No man in his senses can suppose
that the country can for a century to come be governed by a
totally unfrenchified government. If a British Canadian de-
sires to conquer, he must 'stoop to conquer'. He must make
friends of the French without sacrificing the status of his race
or religion. He must respect their nationality. Treat them as a

nation and they will act as a free people generally do—call them a faction and they become factious."

Politics required large amounts of time. As he advanced politically, Macdonald declined professionally. His law practice was neglected. This resulted in a considerable loss of professional income and produced another of Macdonald's perpetual problems: poverty. Never during his political career was he well off. His expenses were high: medical bills alone required huge sums of money, and he enjoyed travel and gracious living. Debt was the result. For most of his political career he owed considerable sums of money, which added to the pressures under which he lived. When tensions became too great he drank. Heavy drinking was a habit that stayed with Macdonald for most of his life.

Occasionally the gloom that hung over his personal life lifted. In March 1850, after great suffering, Isabella gave birth to a second son, Hugh John. His father was enchanted. "We have got Johnnie back again almost his image," he wrote Moll. "I don't think he is so pretty, but he is not so delicate. He was born fat and coarse." As if to counterbalance good fortune and happiness, Charles Stuart, one of Macdonald's dearest friends, died a few weeks later. John A. moaned: "The rod cannot be always smiting."

In 1852 Moll Macdonald married the Rev. James Williamson, a professor at Queen's University. Macdonald was pleased, for his sister was happy and he was fond of "the parson", as he usually called Williamson. The marriage also provided a new centre of family stability, which eased some of the burden carried by John A.

The Census of 1851 had proved that Canada West possessed the larger population. George Brown, the young editor of

Isabella Macdonald

John A. Macdonald, 1858

the *Globe*, Toronto's chief Liberal newspaper, realized the political possibilities of that fact and demanded representation by population. Brown kept the rep-by-pop issue before the public through the columns of the *Globe* and, from 1851 on, through speeches in Parliament, where he was recognized as Canada's most important Liberal leader after 1854. French Canadians, seeing a threat to their influence, opposed rep-by-pop. The issue became crucial to Canadian politics and, like the seat-of-government question, could not be solved easily.

A veritable political revolution occurred in 1854 when Premier Hincks was disgraced after he was caught in a very simple and lucrative swindle. The members of the cabinet, said Macdonald, "are all *steeped to the lips in corruption*; they have no bond of union but the bond of common plunder." The Liberal government was rocked, the Liberal Party divided between the moderates (supporters of Hincks) and the radical groups (Clear Grits and followers of George Brown). Hincks dissolved the House and held a general election and Macdonald piled up another big majority in Kingston. The general results, however, were not definite because the Liberal Party was split into opposing factions. Once Parliament met, it became obvious that Hincks was through. He resigned in September and Allan MacNab was asked to become Premier of the Province of Canada and to form a new government.

MacNab, anxious to gain power, accepted the challenge but Macdonald did the real work of forming the new government. Because of the lack of province-wide parties, coalitions were the order of the day. John A., who did the hard work of cabinet building, was able to combine very different elements in the cabinet: French Canadians who had earlier followed LaFontaine, Canada-West Liberal followers of Baldwin and

Hincks, ultra-Tories like MacNab, and moderate Conservatives like himself. His conciliatory attitude towards the
French made the venture successful. Unknown even to those
involved, the formation of this cabinet was one of the most
important acts in Canadian history. The Coalition of 1854
hardened into a permanent party and was the origin of the
Progressive Conservative Party, known in the last century as
the Liberal-Conservative Party. Slowly and methodically Macdonald, the real power in the coalition, was building one of
Canada's great national political parties.

In the new government Macdonald was Attorney-General
for Canada West, a post of leadership he occupied for many
years. Real power had finally come to him at a time when he
was ready. In spite of his relative youth (he was thirty-nine),
he was a seasoned, matured politician. He had cabinet experience and for ten years had survived in the politics of the
Union. Wit and urbanity helped Macdonald to charm even his
political enemies. Like many nineteenth-century politicians
he loved the bar-room, effectively using conviviality as a
political tool. "[I] dare say you are very busy from *night*
until *morning*," Alexander Campbell remarked in a letter,
"and then again from noon 'til night. The drinking of the
refractory members is in your department, I take for granted—another glass of champagne and *a story of doubtful
moral tendency* with a little of the Hon. John A. Macdonald's
peculiar sawder*—are elements in the political strength of a
Canadian ministry not to be despised, as I have no doubt all
parties in the House are fully aware." Political management
and parliamentary leadership came easily to him as he
worked with zest and efficiency.

The new coalition, with its large majority, quickly solved a
* Flattery, blarney.

series of difficult old problems, although it could not handle
a number of new issues. George Brown campaigned for rep-
by-pop. When he failed to get it he raised the cry that the
government was dominated by the French. Racism entered
the picture, resulting in bitterness and political brutality.

The coalition was strengthened in 1855 when George
Etienne Cartier joined the cabinet. Cartier was a great politician who became Macdonald's co-leader. (It was customary
during these years for governments to be led by co-leaders,
one English- and one French-speaking. The Macdonald-
Cartier partnership was the most successful of these leadership teams.) Their political partnership was highly effective
and lasted until Cartier's death in 1873. MacNab became a
difficult problem. Several members of the cabinet detested
him so much that his presence threatened the stability of the
régime. The issue came to a head in 1856 when Sir Allan
MacNab was deposed as premier and forced out of the
cabinet. Macdonald had been the real leader for some time; in
1856 he was openly recognized as the leader of the Canada-
West Conservatives and the strongest member of the government. As a member of the Assembly noted when MacNab
was deposed, "You have got rid of the King of Trumps, but
you still hold the Knave." Macdonald, "the Knave", reached
the top of what Benjamin Disraeli called the "greasy pole" on
November 26, 1857 when he was appointed titular premier in
the Macdonald-Cartier government.

A general election was held in December 1857. Like most
elections of the period it was marred by violence and fraud.
So public was dishonesty that Conservative managers copied
hundreds of obviously false names into the Quebec City poll
books, including such improbable voters as British Prime
Minister Lord Palmerston, Napoleon I, President George

George Etienne Cartier

Washington, the Duke of Wellington, Judas Iscariot, and Julius Caesar! In the Canada-West riding of Russell the Conservative candidate won after his managers listed 300 false names in the poll books: the names were simply copied from the city directories of several towns in up-state New York. Losing candidates often contested such blatant dishonesty by attempting to have the winners unseated. Such cases, however, were not tried before judges but before parliamentary committees. The majority on such a committee usually supported members of the same party whether or not they had won election through fraud. Racial and religious bigotry also entered the campaign. In the riding of South Ontario, Liberals proclaimed the choice: "Mowat and the Queen" or "Morrison and the Pope".

No pleasure could be taken from the results. The Liberal Party swept Canada West while Conservatives won heavily in Canada East. Each section had sixty-five seats. If Canadian politics became sectionalized the obvious result would be political deadlock, which the leaders feared. For Macdonald personally the election was his most spectacular triumph. Poor John Shaw, the Liberal candidate in Kingston, received seven votes to 1,189 for John A. Macdonald!

Personal triumph could not bring more than limited and temporary satisfaction in 1857; nothing more was allowed by the bleakness of Macdonald's family life. The government's move from Quebec City to Toronto in 1855 had permitted him to re-unite his family. Isabella and Hugh John settled down in Toronto and for a time family life was pleasantly regular. The inevitable blow came early in 1856 when Isabella's terrible illness returned. She declined and became progressively weaker after she was moved back to Kingston. Harassed, overworked, and sick with worry, Macdonald could do nothing but wait for the end. On December 28, 1857, Isabella died in Kingston. A long agony had finally ended, but that was little comfort for Premier Macdonald. He had loved his wife passionately and had lost her.

3

Failure of the Union

Canada has never produced a more wily politician than John A. Macdonald. His skill became proverbial during his own day. In August 1858 Macdonald carried out his most famous political trick, which illustrates magnificently both his tactical skill and his political daring. The seat-of-government question had vexed Canadian politics since 1849. Canada West opposed Quebec City while Canada East opposed any town in Canada West, especially Toronto, and everybody agreed that the temporary solution of alternating the capital between Quebec City and Toronto was completely unsatisfactory. Regular moves every four years produced hopeless confusion. Records were lost; cabinet ministers' families were uprooted; housing became a chronic problem; civil servants felt uncertain and confused. A permanent capital was urgently needed.

Macdonald and Cartier finally found a solution by referring the question to Queen Victoria. She chose Ottawa because for the Province of Canada it was both centrally located and far enough from the American frontier to be safe from attack from American troops. While unable to agree on any other city, most Canadians disliked Ottawa. Goldwin Smith expressed a widely held view when he described Ottawa as a "sub-arctic lumber-village converted by royal mandate into a political cockpit". When Macdonald announced the "Queen's Choice" in February 1858, the Opposition became very angry. A resolution disagreeing with the decision was moved (though no alternate site was suggested), which supporters of Kingston, Quebec City, and Toronto combined to carry, thereby defeating the government of Macdonald and Cartier. This was the beginning of the incident known as the "double shuffle".

Following their defeat, Macdonald and Cartier took stock of their government's position and decided to resign. They almost certainly knew that their position was still strong. The Opposition was disunited and could agree only on its dislike of Macdonald and Cartier. The Conservative leaders in fact were very carefully preparing a trap for the Liberals.

Governor-General Edmund Head asked George Brown, the most prominent of the Liberals, to form a government, which he quickly did. According to the law of the day, a newly appointed minister automatically lost his seat in Parliament and was required to face his constituents at a by-election. So Brown and his ministers were out of Parliament as soon as they were sworn into office as members of the cabinet.

Had the Conservatives adhered to normal parliamentary manners, they would then have agreed to a recess of several weeks to permit the new ministers to hold the required by-elections and prepare a policy statement. But Macdonald had no intention of allowing manners to interfere with politics. He delivered the *coup de grâce* to Brown and his ministry by easily defeating the absent government in Parliament.

Brown now had two choices. He could resign office or call a general election. Deciding on the latter alternative, he asked Governor-General Head to dissolve Parliament. Head, point-

ing to the fact that an election had been held in December
1857, refused. Brown was left with no choice but resignation.
He and his hapless colleagues were out. His two-day government was the shortest in Canadian history.

Governor-General Head, obviously a Conservative supporter, wanted to appear fair. Consequently the new government was formed by Cartier instead of Macdonald. The
Macdonald-Cartier government now became the Cartier-
Macdonald government.

At this point the plot thickens. Macdonald and his associates were anxious to avoid Brown's fate: they had no desire
to face by-elections. Now began the "shuffles". According to
the Independence of Parliament Act (1857), to move from
one cabinet position to another without a by-election was
legal, provided that not more than a month passed between
resigning the first post and taking up the second. The spirit
and intent but not the letter of the Act was to avoid by-elections every time there were minor cabinet changes.

Macdonald immediately realized the implications of the
situation. He arranged for the Conservative cabinet ministers
who had been defeated in the Assembly by Brown to return
to office, but not to their old posts. Because only a short
time had passed since they had lost power, they were not
obliged to face by-elections provided that they were sworn
into new positions. That was the first shuffle. Now came the
truly audacious stroke. After less than an hour in his new job,
each minister resigned and assumed his old post. That was
also legal under the Independence of Parliament Act and was
the double part of the shuffle. Because it was technically,
according to the letter of the law, a cabinet shuffle, by-elections were not required for these ministers. James Young, a
Liberal, described the scene: "The members of the Cabinet

met in a body shortly before twelve o'clock midnight of the 6th August, took the customary oaths to perform the duties of certain departments in the Government which they had no intention of holding, and fifteen minutes after that witching hour [which of course was legally the next day] they were transferred back again to the departments they held prior to their resignations, solemnly swearing again to properly perform the duties appertaining to them."

Brown and his associates were out of office and out of Parliament fighting by-elections; Macdonald, Cartier, and company were comfortably back in their old places. It is easy to understand why John A. Macdonald was hated by his opponents and loved by his friends. During his lifetime he was aptly described as "The Wizard of the North".

John A. Macdonald and George E. Cartier were back in power, but they might well have asked themselves, "So what?" The sad truth was that the system of government was approaching total deadlock. Equal representation from Canada West and Canada East became the most difficult of all problems. In basic terms the Union of 1841 proved to be too restrictive for the dynamic and youthful society of Canada West. Its wishes could too easily be thwarted by the *bloc* of Canada-East M.P.s, which, though exactly the same size as the Canada-West group, represented a section whose interests were often different from those of Canada West.

George Brown demanded representation by population in an attempt to win for his section a preponderance of power in the Union. Such a victory would enable the Brownite Liberals to impose their will in such areas as education, westward expansion, choice of a capital, railway subsidies, and taxation. Canada West was the wealthier section and resented having to pay a major share of taxes spent by a

Conservative government that was increasingly dependent on the Canada-East *bloc* for its existence. (Forgotten was the fact that Canada East was forced to assume a share of Canada West's public debt when the Union was organized in 1840-1.) The politicians of Canada East were strongly opposed to representation by population because to them, equal representation was an essential guarantee of their French-Canadian identity.

Westward expansion into the prairie lands controlled by the Hudson's Bay Company was a vital concern of the Liberals. Canada, argued the *Globe* in 1856, "is fully entitled to possess whatever parts of the great British American territory she can safely occupy." This view was regarded with deep suspicion by the French leaders, who believed (correctly, as it turned out) that the Northwest would be colonized by Ontario, further weakening the position of Lower Canada.

As time passed, Canada West felt increasingly restricted and frustrated by the Union. Many people there became bitter about the fact that the dominant political party was centred in French Canada. Consequently racism tended to become one of the most obvious characteristics of Canadian politics. People in Canada West often blamed French Canadians for their political defeats. An 1863 comment by the Toronto *Globe* illustrates this point: "We . . . urge that every opportunity may be given for the just settlement of the Representation question, and the opening of the great Northwest, for sectional reasons. But those matters have their provincial . . . aspects too. We do not desire to see Canada financially ruined. We do not want to see her progress hindered by the continued domination of a power the highest of whose aspirations is the conservation of everything French." In one anti-French-Canadian tirade the *Globe* thundered: "If

Upper Canada was only united, French Canada's power would be at an end."

Regional and racial conflict, then, threatened to destroy the Province of Canada. The Union was becoming sectionalized; the Liberals were dominating Canada West and the Conservatives were controlling Canada East. Equal sectional representation in Parliament made stable government impossible. Governments came to lack what was called a "drinking majority". That is, parties were so evenly balanced that if a handful of government supporters went out for a drink, the government might be defeated in Parliament and fall.

By the early 1860s creative legislation was impossible and strong government was a thing of the past. Macdonald became disgruntled and unhappy, as did most other politicians. Petty squabbles combined with mean invective were all too common. Personal complications intensified John A.'s unhappiness. With Isabella dead he was very much alone. If he was not pursuing politics he was at his rooming house or drinking with his cronies. Hugh John, still a lad, remained in the care of relatives. Macdonald became unhappy and irritable with his drab and difficult existence. In April 1861 he was criticized in Parliament by his former law student, Oliver Mowat. John A. lost his temper. "You damned pup," he shouted, "I'll slap your chops!" Had John Sandfield Macdonald not separated the two men, a fist fight would have ensued. Macdonald's mind lingered on retirement and he began to consider leaving political life in order to rebuild his law practice and re-unite his family.

An election was held during the spring and early summer. Seeking revenge for his humiliation, Oliver Mowat tried to win Kingston away from Macdonald in an election that was punctuated with violence and marred by bitterness. Nonetheless Macdonald won an easy victory. His candidates did well throughout Canada West, though Conservative gains there were offset by losses in Canada East. Government forces were once again evenly balanced against the Opposition. The parliamentary situation had not changed at all and complete deadlock was fast approaching.

A vital new problem now confronted the Canadian leaders. On April 12, 1861 the American Civil War began when southern guns opened fire on Fort Sumter. This sad event had some grim possibilities for Canada. If Britain entered the Civil War, Canada, which was part of the British Empire, would automatically be involved. Official circles in Great Britain tended to support the Confederate South. British involvement, if it came, would mean war with the North.

Canadians also feared that if the North won the war it might use its victorious armies for the conquest of Canada. This concern prompted D'Arcy McGee's remark: "They coveted Florida, and seized it; they coveted Louisiana, and purchased it; they coveted Texas, and stole it; and then they picked a quarrel with Mexico, which ended by their getting California. They sometimes pretended to despise these colonies as prizes beneath their ambition; but had we not had the strong arm of England over us, we should not have had a separate existence." At any time an incident could start a war. For five long, painful years Canadian leaders faced this daily possibility. For Macdonald the Civil War brought the usual fear, but it also confirmed some of his values. "The fratricidal conflict now unhappily raging in the United States", he told a Kingston audience, "shows us the superiority of our institutions, and of the principle on which they are based. Long may that principle—the monarchical principle—prevail in this land."

Great Britain controlled Canadian foreign policy and was responsible for Canadian defence. But Britain's responsibilities were as far-flung as her enemies. She expected Canada to make some contribution to her own defence, and many Canadians, including Macdonald and Cartier, agreed. In May 1862 the government acted. Macdonald asked Parliament to pass a new Militia Bill. By today's standards it was a modest affair, but it offended two groups of M.P.s. The Opposition objected to the cost; some French-Canadian Conservatives, suspicious of any participation in "English" wars, agreed. To complicate matters Macdonald failed to give real leadership. Instead he went on a prolonged bout of drinking. As Donald Creighton explains in his great biography of Macdonald: "He was drinking heavily; and he went on drinking heavily in complete and cheerful disregard for the Militia Bill, the Canadian government, the Conservative Party, and the military necessities of the British Empire." The result was the fall of the government following an adverse vote in the House. It was just as well. Excluding George Brown's two-day régime in 1858, Macdonald had been in power since 1854. Eight years in office is a long time. John A. needed time to rest and think. He needed to earn money and to spend time with his son. He told Moll that defeat was welcome: "I am at last free, thank God, and can now feel as a free man."

Macdonald, at forty-seven, was still a fairly young man in 1862. He had been in public life for eighteen years. There is little doubt that when the government fell he considered retirement seriously. But politics were a way of life for nineteenth-century politicians. Careers were long; public men were usually tenacious. It is not surprising that Macdonald's attitude changed. Sitting in opposition as leader of the Canada-West Conservatives, he was confronted by an ineffectual government lacking in courage and imagination. The new premier, John Sandfield Macdonald (not related to John A.), was a prickly individualist with a penchant for procrastination and pithy, often unfortunate, remarks. A few years later, for example, when he was the first premier of Ontario, he replied to political opponents who wanted a special favour for the town of Strathroy: "What the hell has Strathroy done for me?"

John A.'s political instincts were soon aroused. This government had to go. He bided his time until May 1863 when he knew that the administration was doomed. A want-of-confidence motion was then carried 64-59. Sandfield Macdonald had one remaining chance of saving himself. He asked the Governor-General to dissolve Parliament. Mr Head obliged. The following elections sustained Sandfield Macdonald's government but completed parliamentary deadlock. Government and Opposition were so closely balanced that a handful of independent members could make or break a government at will.

This ridiculous situation continued until December 1863 when an opportunity arose to test the government's popularity—and perhaps take away its majority. A.N. Richards, M.P. for South Leeds, was made Solicitor-General. According to the law he returned to his constituents for re-election. Macdonald was determined that Richards should lose. During January 1864 South Leeds was a political battleground of considerable importance. Macdonald stumped the county with D'Arcy McGee, who was an important Irish-Catholic leader. McGee had been a member of Sandfield Macdonald's government but had been dismissed during a major cabinet shuffle earlier in 1863. He then joined the Conservatives and became one of Macdonald's most famous lieutenants. For the two important Conservatives it was a happy conflict. During the day they campaigned and at night they ate and drank. After settling in for the evening, which always involved several stiff drinks, they led sing-songs. One of their favourite ditties ended with the refrain: "A drunken man is a terrible curse/But a drunken woman is twice as worse."

Albert Norton Richards proved a victim of this merry time. He lost his seat and Sandfield Macdonald lost his majority. Though the government was inept, Sandfield Macdonald himself was a hard realist: he resigned in March before the Conservatives could defeat him in the House.

What now? The majority of Macdonald and Cartier was as slender as that of Sandfield Macdonald. Were they forever to play the old game by the old rules? Was another unstable government to be formed? Many hoped not. Talk of a coalition was common. Even Macdonald was willing to step aside if a new leader could be found to build a stronger government. None could. For over a week the Province of Canada had no government. Then another purely Conservative administration was formed. Dr Etienne Taché was titular leader, but Macdonald and Cartier were in fact back in power. The Taché-Macdonald government, as it was called, was formed on March 30, 1864. Ten weeks later, on June 14, it was defeated. Deadlock was now complete: no government could hope to stay in power. It was clear to everybody that the constitution of the Province of Canada was dead. If Macdonald could not make the machinery of the Union work, who could? A fresh approach was needed.

4

Confederation

A political revolution solved the problem of deadlock. Unknown to the Canadian public, preparations were well underway for the most momentous event in Canadian history—the confederation of all British North America into a new nation. Existing in some version as early as the Conquest, the idea of confederation regularly came to the fore at times of crisis. Lord Durham canvassed the idea in his famous *Report*. During the annexation crisis of 1849 many moderate Conservatives, including Macdonald, argued for confederation instead of annexation to the United States. The Cartier-Macdonald government, when it was restored to power after the "double shuffle" of 1858, endorsed the idea. It was not surprising that the scheme became popular again during the political deadlock of the 1860s.

In spite of his flirtation with confederation in the British North American League of 1849, and in 1858, John A. was not a warm advocate of any revolutionary plan that would disturb the Union of 1841. He made his position clear in 1861: "If I had any influence over the minds of the people of Canada, any power over their intellect, I would leave them this legacy: 'Whatever you do adhere to the Union—we are a great country, and shall become one of the greatest in the universe if we persevere; we shall sink into insignificance and adversity if we suffer it to be broken.' God and nature have made the two Canadas one—let no factious men be allowed to put them asunder."

Confederation would bring rep-by-pop. An enlargement of the Canadian union would involve the merging into one country of a large number of English-speaking British North Americans. Important to the confederation movement in Canada West was a desire to acquire the agricultural lands of the Northwest. All these changes could threaten French-Canadian authority and culture. Consequently French Canadians viewed confederation with deep suspicion and their hostility naturally influenced Macdonald. After all, the power of the Macdonald-Cartier alliance depended upon French-Canadian votes.

The man responsible for making confederation a practical policy was Macdonald's bitterest and most detested enemy, George Brown. He and Macdonald disliked each other both as men and as politicians. Their hatred dated back to the late 1840s when George Brown, as a member of an investigating commission, secured the dismissal of Macdonald's friend Henry Smith Sr as Warden of Portsmouth Penitentiary (then a few miles west of Kingston). The quarrel festered for years, finally erupting in 1856 when Macdonald publicly charged that Brown "had falsified evidence . . . that he had pardoned convicts, and that he had pardoned murderers that they might give evidence against Warden Smith." So bitter was the relationship that they would not speak to each other outside of Parliament. To John A. Macdonald, George Brown, both "dishonest" and "dishonourable", was simply a "scoundrel". Macdonald's view of Brown was highly unfair for the Liberal leader was an honest and upright man, Canada West's most important Liberal leader and a major force in Canadian

George Brown

politics. He was Macdonald's most effective opponent, which doubtless accounts for much of Macdonald's unreasonable venom.

George Brown was in many ways Macdonald's opposite and their intense mutual hatred was perhaps not surprising. A journalist by profession, Brown had none of Macdonald's devotion to politics. He wanted "justice" for Canada West, and after this was obtained he would give up politics and make a speedy return to journalism. He distrusted men like Macdonald who made politics a way of life, believing that such an approach led only to compromise and corruption. Brown detested Macdonald's craftiness, flexibility, and political skill. To him such characteristics were simply marks of dishonour. The "double shuffle" had confirmed Brown's belief that Macdonald was a dishonest manipulator. Brown of course was also flexible and pragmatic, but as a political craftsman he could never match his opponent. A professional politician and *bon vivant*, Macdonald loved crowds, enjoyed the company of all kinds of men, and relished the parry and thrust of parliamentary debate, while Brown never felt comfortable in the rough and tumble of nineteenth-century public life. Brown was no extreme puritan, but he was moderate compared to John A. and openly criticized Macdonald's drinking habits. Not that such criticism worried Macdonald very much. At one meeting he pointed out: "I know enough of the feeling of this meeting to know that you would rather have John A. drunk than George Brown sober."

Brown, the "human steam-engine", had no inclination for the relaxed and humorous approach to politics that Macdonald so notably espoused. It was a rare situation in which Macdonald found no humour—particularly at the expense of his drinking. On one occasion (so it is reported) he went into a colleague's constituency to make a speech. Heavy drinking had made him somewhat the worse for wear. While listening to a speech by a Liberal he vomited all over the platform. That embarrassment would have mortified and frightened many politicians, but not John A., who was not fazed in the slightest. He began his speech: "Mr Chairman and gentlemen, I don't know how it is, but every time I hear Mr Jones speak it turns my stomach." A potential disaster was dissolved in a roar of laughter. On another occasion, when D'Arcy McGee had been strongly criticized for excessive drinking, Macdonald went to McGee and said: "McGee, no cabinet can stand two drunkards in it, and *you* have to stop." Parliamentary criticism was often deflected with a joke. "I see", said a Liberal opponent, "that J.A. Wilkinson draws a salary as Inspector of Weights and Measures, but when an election is going he spends his time at that." "He is in favour of good measures," was Macdonald's reply.

By 1864 Brown was not merely a sectional leader but a statesman with national vision. Dedicated to the search for a solution to the ills of Canada West, Brown now understood that a simple sectional victory was impossible. The solution must be a workable system of government that could operate for the benefit of Lower as well as Upper Canada. Brown was convinced that confederation was the answer. Parliament gave Brown permission to form a select committee for the purpose of investigating methods of solving the constitutional problems then confronting the Province of Canada. On June 14, 1864, the very day on which the Taché-Macdonald government fell, Brown reported that his committee strongly supported "changes in the direction of a Federative system applied either to Canada alone, or to the whole British North American provinces."

John A. Macdonald, 1863. By William Notman.

The ultimate crisis of Canadian statesmanship was at hand. The Union was bankrupt, the government of the day had fallen, a select committee had recommended fundamental change. Could the leaders rise to the occasion?

George Brown's solution was a grand coalition designed to carry out confederation of all British North America, including the Northwest. Macdonald, who voted against the select committee's recommendation, was lukewarm and considered yet another election. But what, argued Lord Monck, Governor-General of Canada since 1861, was the point? The old system was dead. Elections in 1861 and 1863 had failed to produce stable majorities. Tremendous pressure was applied to Macdonald and Cartier, who finally agreed to a coalition with the Upper Canadian Reformers with a view to carrying out confederation. They really had no choice, as Macdonald explained later: "As leader of the Conservatives in Upper Canada, I then had the option of forming a coalition government or of handing over the administration of affairs to the Grit [Liberal] party for the next ten years." Macdonald had long opposed any basic constitutional change. His party was heavily dependent upon French-Canadian support, and French Canadians preferred the system of government established by the Union of 1841. French Canadians wanted neither rep-by-pop nor confederation and Macdonald agreed. But by June 1864 the old constitution had failed. Basic change was necessary. If Macdonald refused to help produce a new system of government he would be swept aside and the Liberals would take office in order to carry out the needed reforms. Once he saw that change of some sort was inevitable, he shifted his position and agreed to form a coalition to carry out a confederation. He loved power too much to hand over the administration of affairs to anybody else.

Under the nominal leadership of E. P. Taché, the confederation coalition was formed. An amazing government, it was dominated by Macdonald, Cartier, Brown, McGee, and Alexander Galt. Although a late convert to the cause, John A. Macdonald now turned into the movement's most important advocate and architect. He devoted all of his audacity, political skill, national vision, and constitutional genius to the struggle that was to test and utilize every one of his abilities.

Once formed the new cabinet immediately began discussions of a federal union and in a short period worked out a rough outline of the constitution that governs Canada to this day. The question was how to present the plan to the Maritime leaders.

Luck intervened. For years Maritimers, especially in New Brunswick and Nova Scotia, had carried on a vague discussion of Maritime union. For a variety of reasons it was again in the air, but interest was so lukewarm that in spite of months of discussion no serious plan had been made to confer on the matter. At precisely this point Canada asked permission to attend any conference called to consider Maritime union. Macdonald and his colleagues wanted to present *their* scheme. A conference was speedily arranged to meet at Charlottetown, Prince Edward Island, on September 1, 1864, and the Canadian leaders were invited to present their case.

Luck was with the Canadians in the fall of 1864. Weeks before, in August, D'Arcy McGee led 100 Canadian journalists, politicians, and business leaders on a brilliantly successful excursion to the Atlantic colonies. Their object was to study the area with a view to business expansion and improved relations between Canada and the Maritimes. They were welcomed at Saint John, New Brunswick, by 10,000 citizens, and were treated to a twelve-course dinner. Liquor

flowed, songs were sung, and conversations extended long
into the night. Canadians and Maritimers had lived in isolation from each other for decades. At last they were learning
to be friends.

But the Charlottetown Conference remained the really
great event. Canada's leaders were determined to be well
prepared for that crucial meeting and during the summer of
1864 met regularly to discuss and polish the confederation
proposals. These meetings were not always amicable. Late in
August, for example, John A. turned up a bit drunk and had
a nasty quarrel with Brown. Things were patched up, however, and on August 29, 1864 the Canadian delegation de-
parted from Quebec City. All the leading cabinet ministers
sailed in the government-owned *Queen Victoria*. With a
sound and experienced knowledge of how to make confer-
ences work, the Canadians took with them a large store of
champagne.

Prince Edward Islanders were not really very interested in
either confederation or Maritime union. They were an insular
people, concerned with their own problems. The Charlottetown Conference coincided with Slaymaker's and Nichol's
Olympic Circus, which was by far the more popular of the
two affairs.

On September 1, 1864 the *Queen Victoria* anchored off
Charlottetown, where arrangements for meeting the visitors
were somewhat chaotic. Delegated as a one-man reception
committee was W. H. Pope, Provincial Secretary of Prince
Edward Island. Not anticipating the Canadian decision to
anchor off-shore, he was caught unprepared, with no dinghy.
But Pope was a resourceful man and borrowed an oyster boat
from a friendly fisherman. He was rowed out to the *Queen*

Victoria and the Canadian delegates were officially welcomed to the Charlottetown Conference.

The importance of this meeting cannot be over-emphasized. Macdonald, Cartier, Brown, and Galt—the big guns of the Canadian delegation—outlined their confederation scheme in a series of addresses to the conference. They were able, convincing men, but speeches were not enough. Equally important was the social aspect of the conference and John A. stood out brilliantly because of his wit, conviviality, and charm. There is much truth in the suggestion that confederation was floated through on champagne. At Charlottetown the entertainments were gargantuan. Banquets, balls, luncheons, dinners, and drinking sessions, combined with endless political talk, dominated the social scene. These sessions clinched matters. Friendships were formed that ripened into political allegiances. Enthusiasm was generated that gave the leaders the courage needed to carry confederation through to a successful conclusion.

The conference later moved on to Halifax, Saint John, and Fredericton. Everywhere the delegates were showered with toasts, speeches, banquets, and parties. It quickly became obvious that Macdonald and his colleagues had carried the day; they had sold the idea of confederation to the Maritime leaders. The Charlottetown Conference was private: the people were not yet part of the movement. But the political leaders had accepted the concept of a Canadian nation stretching from sea to sea and were fast developing into Canadian nationalists.

A second conference was called for Quebec City, then the capital of the Province of Canada, on October 10. Delegates from Newfoundland, Prince Edward Island, Nova Scotia, New Brunswick, and Canada deliberated in the makeshift

Charlottetown Conference, 1 September 1864. John A. Macdonald is seated close to the centre. Cartier, in profile, is on his right. D'Arcy McGee is behind Cartier. Charles Tupper is standing against the column on the extreme left of the picture. Alexander Galt is seated in front of Tupper. George Brown is at the extreme right with one hand on his knee. Leonard Tilley is in front of the column on Macdonald's left, facing the camera.

parliament buildings on the magnificent heights above the St Lawrence River. This was John A. Macdonald's conference. It was he who drafted most of the resolutions that put into concrete form the abstract principles accepted at Charlottetown, and it was he who moved the first resolution, which stated the chief principle of the new constitution: "The best interests and present and future prosperity of British North America will be promoted by a Federal Union under the Crown of Great Britain, provided such Union can be effected on principles just to the several Provinces."

The five colonies represented had diverse, sometimes opposed, interests. It soon became evident that Newfoundland was not really interested in federal union. Little Prince Edward Island became increasingly annoyed with the new draft constitution, fearing that it would be submerged and lose its identity unless given special privileges. This the other delegates were unwilling to provide for. In spite of these difficulties the work went on under Macdonald's practised guidance, and by October 27 a draft constitution had been accepted by Canada, Nova Scotia, and New Brunswick. It was embodied in the Seventy-Two Resolutions—the basis of the British North America Act of 1867. Canada's constitution had been drafted in a scant two and a half weeks! For over a century it has been a serviceable and flexible constitution.

Macdonald—conciliator, negotiator, and first-class debater—was a superb conference leader. His were the talents that were needed at a private conference where oratory would annoy and inflexibility would prevent reasonable agreement.

Appalling weather marred those two momentous weeks. Constant rain prevented the delegates from getting to know Quebec City and its surrounding countryside. The endless rain in no way hindered social activity, however. The Maritimers, expecting to have a good time, had brought with them their wives and daughters and were not disappointed by the feasts, balls, parties, dinners, receptions, and private drinking sessions. The insatiable nineteenth-century appetite for toasts and speeches was appeased. Wine flowed freely and often. Champagne was a common beverage; bars, private as well as public, were always busy. Maritime families were introduced to Quebec society and presented to Governor-General Monck at his official residence, Spencer Wood.

Macdonald was as skilful on social occasions as he was in conference. He drank with the men and danced with the women. He saw that introductions were made and that nobody went thirsty. It is a marvel that the participants were able to absorb such a massive diet of politics and parties; but they not only survived it, they continued it after October 27! When the Quebec Conference broke up, many delegates proceeded west through Montreal and Upper Canada for more speeches, toasts, and dinners. Canadians and Maritimers were fired with enthusiasm for their new country.

The following months were hectic and difficult. Badly overworked, occasionally ill, and subjected to unreasonable pressure, John A. needed rest and quiet, which he could not have. The confederation movement was under way and problems had to be solved as they arose.

Hostility from the United States was developing into a real menace. The Civil War was drawing to a close with certainty of northern victory. Anglo-American relations were touchy, chiefly because of American resentment about British attitudes towards the South. Although Britain did not enter the Civil War on the side of the South, it was well known in the United States that many leading Englishmen sympathized with the cause of the Confederate states. As Anglo-American relations deteriorated, the American government became more threatening to Canada. In 1864, for example, Canadians entering the United States were required for the first time in history to have passports. It also became obvious in that year that the American government planned to cancel the Reciprocity Treaty of 1854. Any minor squabble could touch off an Anglo-American war. Canadians knew that in such an event their country would speedily be occupied by the enormous and seasoned Grand Army of the Republic.

The situation in the Atlantic provinces turned black and depressing. Joseph Howe, the gifted and popular Nova Scotian, led an agitation against confederation, which he called "the botheration scheme". Nova Scotians were a proud, independent people and preferred their quasi-independence as a colony with responsible government to participation in a huge new federation. Consequently they soon came to oppose confederation. Joseph Howe received so much support that Premier Charles Tupper, already a close ally of Macdonald, did not dare submit the Seventy-Two Resolutions to Nova Scotia's Assembly for approval. There was also strong opposition in New Brunswick. Against John A.'s firm advice, Premier L.S. Tilley held a general election on the issue early in 1865. He suffered a stunning, catastrophic defeat. Without New Brunswick there could be no union with Nova Scotia. Prince Edward Island and Newfoundland were island colonies—they could wait. But New Brunswick and Nova Scotia were essential. Many of Macdonald's opponents were convinced that New Brunswick's hostility had destroyed the movement, in spite of continuous firm support from both the British and Canadian governments.

It was in the midst of these dramatic events that confederation and the Seventy-Two Resolutions were discussed in the Canadian Parliament. It was a great debate, the first in Canadian history to be fully recorded and printed. The Confederation Debates got underway in February 1865 and lasted for seven weeks because most of the M.P.s wanted their views recorded and many points were made over and over again. But in the long run it was worth the time and effort. The discussion was so complete that the public was able to obtain a sound understanding of the new constitution.

John A., the recognized leader of the Assembly and Canada's best parliamentarian, made several important contributions to the Confederation Debates. Canada, he argued, could never again face the deadlock of the period before the formation of the Confederation Coalition when, he pointed out, there was a "danger of impending anarchy". Surely a return to that state was impossible. He explained how confederation would strengthen Canada in relation to the United States. "If we are not blind to our present position, we must see the hazardous situation in which all the great interests of Canada stand in respect to the United States." While hoping that there would be no war between the United States and the United Kingdom, he argued that "the two nations may drift into a war ..." and that it "would then be too late ... to think of measures for strengthening ourselves, or to begin negotiations for a union with the sister provinces."

Macdonald believed that the new nation would be a grand and noble achievement. It would be a federal state, designed to avoid excessive provincial power, as many Canadians believed that the American Civil War was caused by an excess of states' rights. On the other hand, Canada's provinces were to have sufficient authority to protect their dearest interests.

This was especially important to French Canadians, who obtained guarantees for their culture and nationality. Canada's powerful central government was to be located in Ottawa, where the present magnificent parliament buildings were already under construction. The Parliament of Canada was to have two houses: the House of Commons, elected by the people and based on representation by population, and the Senate, appointed by the Prime Minister. Strong representation would be given to Canada's different regions regardless of the size of their populations. The old Province of Canada would be divided into two new provinces, Ontario and Quebec. Provision was made for the eventual admission to the union of Prince Edward Island, Newfoundland, Rupert's Land, and British Columbia.

It was a sensible constitution. In almost every detail, observers could detect Macdonald's influence. He had reason to be proud, and was happier still when the Canadian Parliament approved the Seventy-Two Resolutions by a vote of 91 to 33. It could not become law until passed by the British Parliament, but the scheme had easily overcome one major hurdle.

Shortly after the end of the 1865 session Macdonald enjoyed a long-needed rest. Confederation, defence, and other problems required discussions with British leaders. With some of his colleagues Macdonald was able to go to Britain for a few busy and delightful weeks. On one happy occasion McGee, Macdonald, Galt, Brown, and several English friends attended Epsom Downs for Derby Day. After hours of racing and picnicking they left for London by open carriage. Part of the local tradition involved pelting the inhabitants of neighbouring carriages with peas, fired from the kind of peashooter familiar to all little boys. Macdonald delighted in the fun and even the dour George Brown became quite a good shot.

While he was in England, Oxford University awarded John A. the honorary degree of Doctor of Civil Law. Macdonald took pride in the distinction. "This is the greatest honour they can confer", he told his sister, "and is much sought after by the first men." *Dr* John A. Macdonald returned to Canadian soil on July 7, 1865.

Despite bouts of illness during the summer of 1865, Macdonald found neither rest nor peace. Problems had piled up in his absence; crises errupted with startling regularity and he was plunged into activity and intrigue. The coalition was becoming increasingly unstable. It almost broke up when Sir Etienne Taché died on July 30, 1865, because Governor-General Monck asked Macdonald to become First Minister. This infuriated the prickly George Brown. He insisted that he was equal to Macdonald and Cartier and that his equality must be preserved. The only way to keep Brown happy was to appoint another titular leader under whom Cartier, Macdonald, and Brown could serve as equals. Macdonald agreed, and a figurehead, the unknown and unimportant politician Sir Narcisse Belleau, became Taché's successor as nominal Prime Minister. The coalition was saved, but not for long. In December 1865 Brown left the cabinet. He disliked administration and was annoyed with both John A. and Alexander Galt, the Minister of Finance. Luckily his departure did not provoke a crisis because Brown's devotion to confederation ensured his continued support of the ministry, at least on that issue. Brown's departure relieved Macdonald, for the Toronto editor was a difficult and harping colleague.

The confederation movement had ground to a halt in the Atlantic provinces, but American hostility was Macdonald's most serious concern that summer and fall. Following the end of the American Civil War in 1865, many demobilized soldiers joined an international movement called the Fenian Brotherhood. Fenians were Irish nationalists dedicated to the cause of freeing Ireland from what they regarded as British tyranny. American Fenians considered that attacking Canada would be a fine method of hurting Britain. It is true that the Fenian Brotherhood was a chaotic movement, led by men of hopeless judgement. But because many Fenians were seasoned veterans of the Civil War, possessing guns, ammunition, and money, they posed a very real threat to Canada. Even more alarming, the brotherhood was clearly encouraged by some sections of the American administration. This was an old story for Macdonald, the man who in 1838 had given legal advice to Nils von Schoultz. Macdonald knew all about American "liberation movements"—they were simply fronts for U.S. aggression.

For months Canadians and New Brunswickers lived in terror of Fenian attacks. As it turned out the Fenians were weaker than people believed, although at the Battle of Ridgeway (only a few miles from Niagara Falls) on June 2, 1866 under Colonel John O'Neill they managed to kill nine Canadians and wound thirty others. It was widely and correctly assumed that O'Neill and his 1,500 followers could cross the Niagara River into Canada only with the connivance and support of U.S. officials.

Strangely enough, the menacing Fenians had a beneficial influence, for they encouraged the growth of Canadian patriotism by showing how hostile and imperialistic Americans could be. Many Canadians were converted to confederation because the Fenian Brotherhood, combined with American hostility, convinced them of the need of a strong and unified country firmly allied with Great Britain.

Confederation's greatest single bottleneck was removed in the spring of 1866. In April the anti-confederation government of New Brunswick was forced to resign and a new election was called almost immediately. It was a bitter struggle and was financed to a considerable extent from outside the province, for it was common knowledge that the anti-confederates received support from groups of Americans who wanted a weak, divided, and vulnerable people on their northern frontier. Macdonald and his colleagues countered by raising tens of thousands of dollars for Leonard Tilley of New Brunswick and his confederate followers. The result was a decisive unionist victory. As a final blessing, Charles Tupper managed to pass a pro-confederation resolution through the Nova Scotia Assembly. The last hurdles had been cleared.

One final conference was required to work out the last details of Canada's new constitution and was to be held in London in the summer of 1866. The Maritime delegates sailed on July 19, but the Canadians did not because Macdonald simply would not go. He was still worried about the Fenians and feared the consequences of the instability that wracked current British politics, but liquor was a more important cause of delay: Macdonald was back on the bottle as excessive work, terrible tension, and illness took their toll. He finally pulled himself together, however, and sailed from New York on November 14. The Maritime delegates had sailed four months earlier. Their fury over this requires no explanation.

The London Conference opened on December 4, 1866. In spite of their extreme annoyance with the Canadians, the Maritime leaders accepted Macdonald as the most important leader in British North America and unanimously elected him

chairman of the conference. Under his expert guidance the
delegates worked quickly to add the final touches to the
federal framework that had been hammered out at Charlottetown and Quebec. There were no major changes, but consti-
tutions are complex and the days sped by.

One important decision was made at London. Macdonald
wanted the new country named the "Kingdom of Canada",
but the British leaders feared that the United States might
resent so obviously monarchical a gesture. Instead of ignoring
the views of bumptious men who interfere in other people's
business, the British rejected Macdonald's proposal. Leonard
Tilley, a deeply religious man, found the answer in the
Seventy-Second Psalm: "He shall have dominion also from
sea to sea, and from the river unto the ends of the earth."
The Fathers of Confederation agreed that the new country
should be called Canada, and that it should extend "from sea
to sea". It therefore remained to style the new confederacy
the "Dominion of Canada". Legal experts took the work of
the Fathers and turned it into a constitution called the
British North America Act. It was passed by the British
Parliament on March 8, 1867. John A. Macdonald's greatest
task was completed.

The London Conference left Macdonald with some spare
time. He used it to alter his personal life in a decisive way.
While strolling down Bond Street one day he met Susan
Agnes Bernard. Agnes, as she was usually called, was "tall,
tawny, and . . . to use the harsh phrase of the day, rather
'raw-boned' and angular." But, according to this observer,
"she possessed a keen wit, a quick perception, a liberal mind
and a certain unselfishness of heart." She was "brilliant and
piquant in conversation, and had no small degree of literary

taste and talent. . . ." John A. knew Agnes slightly, for her brother was Lieutenant-Colonel Hewitt Bernard, one of Macdonald's senior aides. The Bernard family was distinguished and influential. Agnes's father served as Attorney-General of Jamaica. Later the family lived in Canada.

Macdonald must have been pleased with his Bond Street encounter. Although Miss Bernard was twenty-one years younger than the Canadian leader, he courted her with considerable enthusiasm. Before the end of the year Agnes agreed to marry John, and they decided to wed as quickly as possible. They were married on February 16, 1867 at St George's Church, Hanover Square. Several of Macdonald's colleagues were present and the bride was attended by four young Canadian ladies. Agnes's brother Hewitt provided a fine wedding breakfast at the Westminster Palace Hotel. Francis Hincks, whom Macdonald had once described as "steeped to the lips in corruption", proposed the traditional toast to the bride.

Because the British North America Act had not yet passed the British Parliament, there was no time for a real honeymoon. John A. and his bride were able to steal off to Oxford for only a short few days.

The second marriage was a good one. Macdonald had often been unbearably lonely during the decade since Isabella's death. Now he could have something that Isabella had never been able to provide—a normal, stable home life. His new wife loved him. She cared for him and entertained his friends. John A. came to know more contentment than he had experienced for many years.

The newlyweds returned to Ottawa where Macdonald was busier than ever before. Nobody challenged his supremacy within Canada or doubted his right to guide the destiny of

Proclamation of Confederation in Kingston, Ont., 1 July 1867

the new dominion. The British North America Act was to come into force on July 1, 1867. For weeks Macdonald slaved to see that all was ready for the great day, Canada's birthday.

Dominion Day 1867 was magnificent in every respect. The weather was perfect—sunny but not too hot. Ottawa greeted Canada's birthday with a 101-gun salute at midnight. Early the next morning festivities, by no means confined to Ottawa, began with a vengeance. Every city, town, village and hamlet celebrated in its own way. Church bells rang the day in, and many Canadians attended special religious services where they prayed for the success of confederation. The proclamation announcing the birth of the Dominion was publicly read by mayors and reeves, and greeted with more military salutes. Parades were organized, troops reviewed, and band concerts staged for the enjoyment of the citizens. Some cities held games, field days, and picnics. Cricket matches were still popular in 1867, and waterfront towns like Kingston hosted regattas. Horse races prevailed in some areas and, of course, there were the inevitable banquets with their endless courses, toasts, and speeches. Bonfires and brilliant fireworks ended the day.

Some dissent marred the festivities. In Nova Scotia, for example, anti-confederates displayed black drapery and flew their flags at half-mast. But basically it was a happy day, and John A. Macdonald was the hero. Everybody knew that he was to be Canada's first Prime Minister. Because of his pre-eminence he was singled out for special recognition. Not the least of the notable events on that first Dominion Day was the announcement that Macdonald had been made a Knight Commander of the Bath. He was now *Sir* John A. Macdonald.

5

Gristle Becomes Bone

The first confederation government (1867-73) was probably the most active and exciting administration in Canadian history. Between 1864 and 1867 Macdonald and his colleagues had created the Dominion of Canada but, as Macdonald pointed out in 1872, "Confederation is only yet in the gristle, and it will require five years more before it hardens into bone." This hardening process was Macdonald's primary concern.

Immense problems faced the four original provinces of Quebec, Ontario, Nova Scotia, and New Brunswick. New administrations were needed for Ontario and Quebec; the old administration of the Union had to be modified to suit federal needs. Ontario and Quebec required physical links with the Maritime Provinces: the Intercolonial Railway had to be built to unite the St Lawrence valley with the Maritimes. Nova Scotia needed to be reconciled to the new order: it wanted to be released from confederation and threatened to become a festering political sore. The very fact that Canada in 1867 consisted of three regions—Ontario, Quebec, and the Maritime Provinces—peopled by citizens of English, Irish, French, Scottish, and German origin, meant that the success of confederation would require hundreds of compromises.

There were also many external problems. Though Canada did not control her relations with the United States, those relations were crucial. The U.S. had cancelled the Reciprocity Treaty in 1866. Many Canadians believed that their fish, timber, and agricultural produce must be sold in the U.S. if these products were to find a sufficiently large market, and that reciprocity promoted such trade. Canadians wanted easy access to American markets. This was a major concern in 1867 and is a recurring theme in Canadian history.

Anglo-American relations represented another problem. During the American Civil War (1861-5), Britain and Canada were officially neutral. Many Canadians and Britons, like George Brown and John Bright (an influential English liberal politician), supported the North. Many more supported the South, however, and they tended to come from conservative and official quarters. After the Civil War ended, the strong and victorious North remembered that many people in Britain and Canada had wanted the South to win and nursed a feeling of resentment. Canadians feared that ill will between England and the United States might lead to war, with Canada becoming a battleground for British and American armies.

A third problem was created by American interest in the Northwest. Informed Canadians feared that the United States might try to annex the Red River Valley, the Saskatchewan district, or British Columbia. At all costs this had to be prevented, for central Canadians regarded the Far West as their rightful heritage.

There was another area of concern in Canada's desire to expand. Prince Edward Island and Newfoundland remained outside confederation and Canada wanted both these provinces to join. The lands of the Hudson's Bay Company, a giant horseshoe extending from Labrador to the Rockies, needed to be annexed. Finally there was British Columbia. If Canada was to become a Pacific power, that distant colony would have to become a Canadian province.

These were Canada's main problems, for which the first Prime Minister was obliged to find most of the solutions.

Sir John A. Macdonald was equal to the task. A Member of Parliament since 1844, he had served in several cabinets. For years he had co-operated closely with Cartier's French-Canadian Conservatives and as early as 1864 had begun to form political associations with Maritime leaders. Macdonald was not only recognized as the finest politician in the new Dominion; he was the only man able to build a national political party.

The formation of a cabinet was his first task. Macdonald was given complete responsibility by Governor-General Monck, who wrote: "I desire to express my strong opinion that, in future, it shall be distinctly understood that the position of First Minister shall be held by *one* person who shall be responsible to the Governor-General for the appointment of the other ministers, and that the system of dual First Ministers, which has hitherto prevailed, shall be put an end to." Sir John Macdonald was in control.

Putting together Canada's first cabinet was a painful experience. Numerous regional and ethnic groups demanded cabinet representation according to their numbers, but Macdonald wanted no more than thirteen ministers because he believed that a larger number made fruitful discussion and reasonable compromise difficult, if not impossible. After much negotiation and near failure Sir John succeeded in forming Canada's first government. Ontario received five ministers, Quebec four, and New Brunswick and Nova Scotia two each. Presbyterians, Catholics, Anglicans, and Methodists were all represented, as were the French, English, Irish, and Scottish. Able men joined the cabinet but there was no room for Charles Tupper or D'Arcy McGee, both Fathers of Confederation. McGee and Tupper, however, were expected to join the cabinet later as vacancies occurred. Shortly after the cabinet was sworn in, a general election was held in which Conservatives won majorities in Ontario, Quebec, and New Brunswick. The Opposition succeeded only in Nova Scotia, where Joseph Howe's anti-confederates swept the board, with Dr Charles Tupper as the only Macdonald supporter elected from that province. Macdonald now had a strong majority in Parliament and was ready to deal with Canada's problems.

Even before the general election Sir John Macdonald and Sir George Cartier protected their political flanks. They were responsible for the appointment of governments in the new provinces of Ontario and Quebec, and made certain that close allies became the premiers of those key provinces: P. J. O. Chauveau became first premier of Quebec, while John Sandfield Macdonald (once John A.'s foe but now his friend) ruled in Ontario. In order to prove the value of confederation to Nova Scotians and New Brunswickers, Macdonald began the immediate construction of the Intercolonial Railroad. Although not completed until the mid-1870s, the railroad provided employment in the coastal provinces and bound them much more closely to Ontario and Quebec.

Nova Scotia provided Macdonald with his first major crisis. It took the form of a dangerous anti-confederation agitation (growing out of the pre-1867 movement) led by Joseph Howe, the most famous of all Nova Scotians. In the federal and provincial elections of 1867 Nova Scotians had opposed confederation by overwhelming majorities and they continued to oppose it. What was Macdonald to do? Strong public opinion could not be ignored. Compulsion was no long-term solution. Without Nova Scotia there would be no Canada.

Macdonald quickly discovered to his advantage that Nova Scotians had an intense loyalty to Great Britain. During the 1850s and 1860s they had reached their highest point of cultural, social, and economic development. A proud people, they were anxious to remain within the British Empire as an internally self-governing colony. If that status was unattainable after 1867, only two alternatives remained: the province could secede from Canada and the Empire and become an American state or satellite or it could accept confederation and remain within Canada.

The first battleground was London. Only the British Parliament, which had made confederation, could release Nova Scotia from its bondage. Joseph Howe, now a member of the Canadian House of Commons, went to London to plead for Nova Scotia's freedom and its pre-1867 position. Macdonald sent Tupper to England to oppose Howe. To the Conservative leaders confederation was a "fixed fact"; they refused to release Nova Scotia from the union or even to negotiate on that point. Macdonald and Tupper won: the British government confirmed confederation and told Howe that he would find no relief in that quarter. This brought Nova Scotian loyalty into the centre of the picture, for Howe knew that if his agitation continued it might get out of hand and lead to Nova Scotia's annexation to the United States.

Howe was determined to avoid annexation, which he regarded as disloyalty to Britain. Only one alternative remained: continued membership in Canadian confederation. By 1869 this was as clear to Howe as it was to Tupper and Sir John. Howe concluded that he had no choice but to come to terms and agreed to negotiate with the federal government. In 1869 the matter was settled. Joseph Howe and his followers in the House of Commons agreed to support both confederation and the government. In return an improved financial deal was made with Nova Scotia, which became the first province to gain "better terms" from Ottawa. The contract was sealed when Howe joined Sir John's cabinet. Nova Scotia was now pacified, though it still was not happy.

Meanwhile, on February 8, 1869 Agnes gave birth to a baby girl. Both mother and child almost died during a long and difficult delivery. But they recovered and Macdonald delighted in watching baby Mary grow. As so often happened to Macdonald, however, a happy personal event quickly developed into a tragic situation. Little "Baboo", as the baby was nicknamed, was not a normal child. She was "a victim of hydrocephalus—an affliction caused by an effusion of water on the brain." Shortly after his child's birth Macdonald understood that a slightly enlarged head combined with slow development would involve for Mary a lifetime of difficulty and frustration. Like his first wife, Macdonald's only daughter would always be a quasi-invalid, both frail and sickly. This abnormal condition seemed to feed Macdonald's protective instincts and he developed a warm affection for Mary.

Part of the confederation agreement allowed for the annexation of the Northwest. Westward expansion was important to Ontario. The Maritimes were given a railroad; Quebec received cultural guarantees; Ontario wanted the West. Before 1864 Macdonald had been tepid about westward expansion; he respected French-Canadian views. After 1867 he was committed to the policy. Delegates were dispatched to London to negotiate with the British government and the Hudson's Bay

Company (which owned Rupert's Land). After long and sometimes unpleasant negotiations, Canada purchased the Northwest in 1869. The Company received 300,000 pounds, some 50,000 acres surrounding its trading posts, and one-twentieth of the land in western Canada's fertile belt. At one stroke Canada acquired an empire that included the Prairies, most of what is now northern Ontario and Quebec, and part of Labrador. Without this purchase modern Canada could never have come into existence.

In all of Rupert's Land there was only one concentrated settlement—the Red River colony, consisting of French Métis, English halfbreeds, Selkirk settlers, Hudson's Bay Company employees, and immigrants from Ontario and the United States. The Red River colony was mature and self-conscious. It contained able men who were determined to join confederation only after entry terms had been carefully negotiated. The leaders of the colony regarded full consultation as their right and knew how to protect their interests. Macdonald neglected to take these people seriously and as a consequence committed one of the gravest blunders of his career.

Provincehood, Macdonald reasoned, was not necessary for the new territories. They could be controlled by the national government and administered by a Lieutenant-Governor under the authority of "An Act for the Temporary Government of Rupert's Land". William McDougall, an Ontario Liberal who supported Sir John, was appointed Lieutenant-Governor of the Northwest Territories. Prejudiced against the French Métis, filled with pride in his position, and ignorant of the conditions that awaited him, McDougall and his retinue moved west. Communications were so primitive that to travel from Ontario to Manitoba it was necessary to go through American territory. After a long and tiring journey, McDougall crossed the forty-ninth parallel at Pembina, a village directly south of Winnipeg. There his way was blocked. On October 21, 1869 he was given a note that read simply: "The National Committee of the Métis of Red River instruct Mr McDougall not to enter the North-West Territory without special permission from this Committee." It was signed John Bruce, President, and Louis Riel, Secretary. McDougall could do nothing; he had no army. He lingered for a time in Minnesota and then returned to Ontario, a broken man.

What had happened and what did it mean? The answer is not very complex. The people of Red River, with the exception of a small pro-Canada party, resented the idea that they could be sold to Canada like a herd of cattle. Confederation might be a fine idea, but westerners wanted to join only after Ottawa negotiated acceptable terms of entry with *them*. While this feeling was general throughout the settlement, it was given form by the French-speaking Métis, led by the charismatic Louis Riel.

The Métis are a great and tragic people. Originally they were the children of French fur traders and Indian women. During the long struggle between the Hudson's Bay Company and the North West Company earlier in the century they became a coherent and powerful force. After they massacred Governor Semple and his men at Seven Oaks in 1816 their power was visible to all. They regarded themselves as a "New Nation", to use their own term. For two generations they lived a rough and boisterous life, but they prospered and for the most part were happy. Able leaders emerged in the Red River valley: Cuthbert Grant, James Sinclair, John Bruce, Louis Riel the Elder, and Louis Riel the Younger. They were

often assisted and influenced by their priests, for the Métis
were a religious people. Twice a year they held a massive
buffalo hunt, organized in military fashion. From this experience came their tough military and political traditions. But
to survive they required a simple society. They were neither
farmers nor speculators. Their most brilliant leader, the
young and college-educated Louis Riel, described their problem when he pointed out to the Council of Assiniboia in
1869 that the Métis were "only half civilized, and felt, if a
large immigration were to take place, they would probably be
crowded out of a country which they claimed as their own."

The Métis had to be protected. Louis Riel and his advisers
were determined to obtain that protection, and at the same
time to speak for other Manitobans. Their plan was simple:
to resist annexation until Canada and the people of Red
River had negotiated terms acceptable to both groups. This
explains why Riel occupied Fort Garry on November 2, 1869
and established a provisional government. Delegates were sent
to Ottawa to conduct the negotiations. The federal government was unusually co-operative because it feared American
intervention. By May 1870 an agreement had been hammered
out and the terms written into the Manitoba Act, which
established the Province of Manitoba.

The first new province was much smaller than it is today,
and in 1870 contained only some 12,000 inhabitants. It was
given responsible government and guarantees for the French
language and the Roman Catholic religion. Manitoba was not
treated like the other provinces. Public lands within the
province were retained by the federal government, for use in
subsidizing a transcontinental railway, and the first two Lieu-
tenant-Governors were given more power than the provincial
politicians. Nonetheless the creation of Manitoba was a great

event, and Louis Riel was chiefly responsible. As he commented in 1885: "I know that through the grace of God I am the
founder of Manitoba."

The new province had not come into being easily. During
the Resistance (or Rebellion, as it is often called) several of
Riel's opponents were jailed at Fort Garry. Thomas Scott was
a particularly unpleasant prisoner. An Orangeman and a
racist, he abused his Métis guards and hurled insults at Riel
whenever possible. In the end he was court-martialled with
the rough justice common to buffalo hunters. Condemned to
death, Scott was taken outside the walls of Fort Garry on
March 4, 1870 and shot by a Métis firing squad. As he was
led to his doom, Scott exclaimed: "This is horrible! This is
cold-blooded murder!" Many Ontario Protestants agreed with
him. To them Scott became a loyal British martyr, murdered
by a French Catholic. As Ontarians became angrier, French
Canadians sprang to Riel's defence. Soon Ontario and Quebec
were seething with discontent, and the question of what to
do about the rebel leaders became an extremely difficult one.
To arrest them would anger Quebec; to pardon them would
antagonize Ontario. Fortunately for Macdonald he was able
to send an Anglo-Canadian military expedition to Red River
in the spring of 1870. When it approached Fort Garry, Riel
fled to exile and Macdonald was spared the problem of
deciding whether to arrest or pardon the Métis chief. The
incident revealed the fragility of confederation. Racial problems could destroy Canada if they were not checked.

The immense Northwest was now annexed and Manitoba
became Canada's fifth province. The Northwest Territories
was made a separate unit governed initially by the Lieutenant-Governor of Manitoba.

At this point Macdonald became seriously ill. On May 6,

Lady Macdonald, 1873

1870 he went as usual to his office in the East Block. A government official, passing his office door, heard a thump. When he investigated he found Sir John "lying on the floor and writhing in agony". E. B. Biggar explained what had happened: "The immediate cause of his sickness had been the passing of a gallstone of unusual size. The agony caused by it had thrown him into convulsions. The stone would not come away, and his nervous force was exhausted by the pain. His utter prostration left the muscles relaxed, and this relaxation let the stone pass away." So ill was the Prime Minister that it was widely assumed that he was dying. For weeks he could not be moved from Parliament Hill. But Macdonald was a tough, spirited man. He started to recover and was finally able to travel to Prince Edward Island, where for a couple of months he recuperated in the sun and fresh air. When he returned home in September he had almost recovered, but not quite. "I am now in very good health", he told his sister, "and *nearly* as strong as before my illness. I hope by care and regular exercise I shall soon regain all my strength. I shall not do much work for some months, but act in the Government as Consulting Physician."

During his illness and in his absence the work of expansion continued. With the Northwest safely annexed, the way to the Pacific was open. British Columbia became the next danger point. That region had been transformed from a fur-trading district to a rough frontier mining colony by the Fraser River gold rush, which began in 1858. Many miners were Americans, and the colony forged numerous ties with the western United States. Some feared that British Columbia might be forced into the maw of the land-devouring country to the south. British Columbia's position as a colony had to change, for she had an absurdly heavy debt; at the same time

Great Britain was losing interest in defending her Pacific-coast colony. B.C. required financial support, a protector, and a communications link with eastern North America. These requirements could be provided in two ways: it could become part of the United States through annexation or it could federate with the new Dominion of Canada. Within the colony both policies had supporters. The result was a vigorous, if brief, debate about the colony's future, which was won by the supporters of confederation led by the colourful Amor De Cosmos (whose original name was William Alexander Smith).

In June 1870 British Columbia and Canada agreed to terms of union. Because of Macdonald's illness, Sir George Cartier handled Canada's negotiations. This agreement was nonetheless crucial to Macdonald's career and reputation. The terms were generous. British Columbia was given responsible government and financial stability; the province was to have six M.P.s, more than its population justified. But the real generosity involved transportation. British Columbia, with a small and declining white population of only 10,586 in 1870, was separated from Canada by 2,000 miles of wilderness. It wanted the immediate construction of a coach road from Red River to the coast. Cartier staggered the delegates by promising a *railroad* to the Pacific within ten years! Canada, with only 4,000,000 people, calmly agreed to construct one of the world's largest railway systems. Needless to say, B.C. immediately ratified the terms and became Canada's sixth province in 1871.

Before leaving office in 1873 Macdonald planned the Royal North-West Mounted Police. The "Mounties" immediately became an important part of western Canadian life. Dressed in scarlet tunics and buff breeches, they brought order and security to Canada's western empire. The force comprised a mere handful of men but it patrolled an area larger than several European countries. As years passed, the Mounties were given national responsibilities and the name of the force was changed to the Royal Canadian Mounted Police. The RCMP is now one of Canada's most famous institutions.

The nation-building work of the first government was not complete. Prince Edward Island was brought into confederation as province number seven in 1873. Sir John Macdonald had thus presided over Canada's growth from a small eastern federation to a gigantic transcontinental nation, stretching from the Atlantic to the Pacific.

External problems confused this period of intense activity. Britain and the United States decided to settle their major differences, which had grown out of problems from the Civil War period. Three Canadian issues were at stake: compensation for the Fenian raids; a substitute for the Reciprocity Treaty that would give Canadian businessmen freer access to the American market; and American demands for access to Canadian-owned deep-sea fisheries. Because the British Empire was a diplomatic unit, these problems were lumped together with those of exclusive interest to the British, and were to be settled by an Anglo-American High Commission in 1871. Owing to the importance of Canadian interests, Sir John A. Macdonald was appointed a member of the five-man British delegation to Washington.

As a delegate of the British Empire and not of Canada, Macdonald was in a difficult position. If, in the process of problem-solving, Canadian interests had to be sacrificed, he would be in political danger at home regardless of the larger issues at stake. As it turned out, Canadian interests *were* sacrificed. The Americans refused to compensate Canada for

damage caused by the Fenians, and the British declined to
press the matter. No important trade concessions were made
to Canada. Finally, the United States convinced the British
that American fishermen should have the right to fish in
Canadian waters. Macdonald was not opposed to such an
agreement, but in return he wanted a trade arrangement that
would open American markets to Canadian produce. All he
got was financial compensation, the amount to be decided by
a team of neutral arbitrators. "Never in the whole course of
my public life", he said, "have I been in so disagreeable a
position and had such an unpleasant duty to perform as the
one upon which I am now engaged here." Sir John was
required to sign the treaty. He then went home to face the
storm.

Macdonald had been involved in the surrender of Canadian
interests. But what could he have done? While it was true
that the Canadian Parliament would have to ratify the sections of the Treaty of Washington concerned with Canada, it
was equally true that the rejection of one section would veto
the entire treaty. The result could be an Anglo-American war
in which Canada would not be neutral. Macdonald thus asked
Parliament to ratify the treaty. The Liberals fumed and raged
but to no avail. The Treaty of Washington was approved by
Parliament in 1872.

In some respects Macdonald's struggle to make the Treaty
of Washington acceptable to Canadian public opinion was his
finest hour. He took the long statesmanlike view of Canada's
best interests, not the short view that might attract regional
or class support. He courted unpopularity because of his
dedication to Canadian survival. "[We] ask the people of
Canada through their representatives", he said in the House
of Commons, "to accept this treaty, to accept it with all its

imperfections, to accept it for the sake of peace, and for the sake of the great Empire of which we form a part." It should also be remembered that Macdonald gained personal prestige by helping to negotiate the Treaty of Washington, for he was a participant in a major diplomatic event.

The election of 1872 presented Macdonald with a host of new problems. Nineteenth-century federal politics were regional in nature. Provincial lieutenants carried the burden in their own provinces: Charles Tupper and Joseph Howe in Nova Scotia; Leonard Tilley and Peter Mitchell in New Brunswick; Hector Langevin and Sir George Cartier in Quebec; Lieutenant-Governor Morris in Manitoba; Amor De Cosmos in British Columbia. The Ontario wing of the federal cabinet was weak and Macdonald was required to carry most of the heavy load of electioneering. The task was enormous for there were eighty-eight seats in Ontario, and the Liberals were well led and aggressive. Macdonald also had to do the work of Prime Minister and give guidance and advice to candidates and leaders throughout the country.

Sir John's government had accomplished a great deal in five years, but the opposition found much to criticize. Nova Scotia's "better terms" were attacked in Ontario. The Treaty of Washington was unpopular in Ontario and the Maritimes. French Canada felt that Riel was treated with excessive severity after the Red River Resistance, while Ontario felt that he was treated too leniently.

The elections were spread over several weeks. This put an additional strain on Macdonald, who rushed from riding to riding to assist his candidates.

The constituency of Centre Toronto illustrates the bitterness and heat of the campaign. A Conservative organizer wrote to a cabinet minister: "We had great excitement yester-

day over the Central Division Election. It is said none of the
old famous struggles were anything like it. The halt, the lame,
the blind, and even the absent and the dead were brought out
to vote . . . and there can be no doubt a large sum of money
was spent, and probably on both sides."

Macdonald and his Conservatives won the election but lost
Ontario. "I had to fight a stern and up-hill battle in Ontario,"
commented Macdonald, "and had I not taken regularly to the
stump, a thing that I have never done before, we should have
been completely routed." Nationally the Conservative majority was not large, and several western and Maritime M.P.s
were shaky supporters.

Difficulties never ceased: one problem merged with another in a blur of action that became a political nightmare.
The next crisis was a disastrous one. It had its roots in
Cartier's promise to build a railroad to the Pacific within ten
years. The fulfilment of this promise was made enormously
difficult because of the conditions Macdonald thought were
essential to the line's success. The Canadian Pacific Railway
Company should not be controlled by United States interests
or it would not fulfil its role as a national unifier. In the
words of Sir George Cartier: "Never will a damned American
company have control of the Pacific." It had to be supported
by the business communities of both Montreal and Toronto
or it would be unable to raise the money necessary for its
construction. Macdonald's plan was to form a company representing both Toronto and Montreal, give it a charter to
build the railroad, and then hold the general election required
by law before the end of 1872.

The plan failed because the capitalists refused to co-operate. Two rich, influential businessmen, Sir Hugh Allan of
Montreal and David Macpherson of Toronto, demanded the

presidency of the firm. Allan was unusually stubborn, and
Macpherson claimed (correctly as it turned out) that Allan
had secretly agreed to sell control to American railroad men.
To complicate matters further, Toronto and Montreal quar-
relled over the site of the line's terminus. Macdonald used all
of his great skills to bring Allan and Macpherson together but
he failed. These delicate and important negotiations were in
progress during the hard-fought election of 1872.

When Parliament opened in 1873, the election became the
most important issue of the year. On April 2, 1873, Lucius
Seth Huntington, Liberal M.P. for Shefford, charged that the
government had sold the CPR charter to Sir Hugh Allan in
return for election contributions during the 1872 campaign.
Thus began the Pacific Scandal, Canada's most famous corruption case. As it turned out, Sir Hugh Allan's firm *had* been
given the charter to build the line; the Conservative Party *had*
been given the enormous sum of $179,000 (equal to about
$895,000 today) during the election; and there was a direct
connection between the two.

Much of Allan's money had gone to George Cartier, who
was required to wage a desperately bitter struggle in his own
riding of Montreal East and on behalf of his candidates
throughout Quebec. Sir George lost Montreal East but was
promptly elected for Provencher, Manitoba. Cartier was seriously ill during the campaign. His judgement was affected
and in accepting huge sums of money from Allan he compromised himself and the government. His illness was diagnosed
as Bright's disease and, critically ill, he went to London to
seek medical attention. On May 20, 1873 the tough, ebullient
little man died. For Sir John the blow was staggering. Cartier
and Macdonald had governed Canada for almost twenty
years. They were co-leaders bound together by two decades

of common experience, affection, and respect. Now Cartier was gone and could not defend himself or the government. The entire burden was thrown on Macdonald. Cartier's funeral on June 13 brought home to Sir John his political isolation. Drinking heavily, the Prime Minister was depressed and bitter. He considered resigning the prime ministership but his colleagues convinced him that only his leadership could prevent the disintegration of the Conservative Party.

The Pacific Scandal rocked Canada. The documents published to prove the Liberal charges were spectacular. The most famous was Macdonald's telegram: "Immediate, private. I must have another ten thousand—will be the last time of calling. Do not fail me; answer today." Sir Hugh Allan's lawyer, J. J. C. Abbott (Conservative M.P. for Argenteuil), immediately replied: "Draw on me for ten thousand dollars." Other evidence was just as spectacular. In July 1872, for example, Cartier wrote to Allan:

Dear Sir Hugh:

The friends of the Government will expect to be assisted with funds in the pending elections, and any amount which you or your company shall advance for that purpose shall be re-couped to you.

A memorandum of immediate requirements is below.

NOW WANTED

Sir John A. Macdonald	*$25,000*
Hon. Mr Langevin	*15,000*
Sir G.E.C.	*20,000*
Sir J.A. (add'l)	*10,000*
Hon. Mr Langevin	*10,000*
Sir G.E.C.	*30,000*

Nobody expected such money to be "re-couped". The fact was that during the course of the election campaign Conservative leaders accepted great sums of money from Allan. Macdonald accepted a total of $45,000, Cartier $85,000, Langevin $32,600, and other Conservative politicians received between $16,000 and $17,000. This money came from a man who was convinced he had been promised the presidency of the CPR! The public drew the obvious conclusion, which was that Macdonald and his colleagues sold control of the CPR to Allan in return for massive campaign contributions.

An American businessman named George McMullen possessed a great quantity of correspondence that incriminated both Sir Hugh Allan and the Conservative Party. He had worked closely with Allan on the railway project but had been dismissed by the devious Montrealer. His dismissal infuriated McMullen and in an attempt to obtain what he regarded as justice he visited Macdonald on New Year's Eve, 1872. McMullen's proposition was perhaps veiled but it was nonetheless simple. The incriminating correspondence would be published unless the American railroad men received justice. Justice was to consist of either the Americans' inclusion in the CPR or Allan's exclusion from the great enterprise. Macdonald refused to be blackmailed, and McMullen consequently sold his evidence to the Liberal Party for a large payment—probably $25,000. Later, Montreal Liberals bribed a clerk in the office of Allan's lawyer to copy additional incriminating evidence. This correspondence was devastatingly effective because the lawyer, J. J. C. Abbott, had handled Allan's election contributions. These documents thus revealed much of the subterranean detail connected with the financing of the Conservatives' campaign in 1872.

It was becoming clear that the Liberal leaders could be as venal as the Conservatives. To collect their evidence the Liberals had worked with blackmailers, swindlers, and thieves, and the Conservatives made as much political capital as they could out of these unsavoury associations. They could not, however, overcome the central stark fact that leading Conservatives had promised Allan the presidency of the CPR *and, at the same time,* accepted from him massive campaign contributions.

A Royal Commission charged with the task of investigating the situation was pro-Conservative, but it nonetheless revealed all the facts to the public. The press of the nation debated the issue; a desperate struggle was waged to gain the loyalties of M.P.s. For Macdonald it was a summer of pure hell. His government, his national programs, his leadership, and his personal reputation were at stake. The frenzy of the opposition press knew no limits. Early in August, for example, it was suggested to Canadians that their Prime Minister had drowned himself in the St Lawrence River! Sir John was further depressed by the fact that public sympathy had swung sharply away from the government. As Governor-General Dufferin commented on August 14: "I don't think the régime can last much longer."

Sir John was back on the bottle, and had been since the election. His cabinet colleague and former law partner, Alexander Campbell, explained to a friend: "We . . . know in the past that Sir John's policy of delay has very often succeeded and we know also how partial he always is to that course, and how difficult it is to persuade him or to bring reasons of sufficient weight to change his views, and also how apt one is to yield one's own judgment to that of a colleague whose ability and political experience are so universally honored. In this particular instance I am persuaded he was haunted by an idea, which turned out to be utterly without foundation, that there were some telegrams behind which would be published and this dread paralyzed his action. I do not believe up to the last moment that he felt sure, or now feels sure, that all he telegraphed during the Elections has come out. From the time he left Kingston, after his own election . . . I am very much afraid he kept himself more or less under the influence of wine, and that he really has no clear recollection of what he did on many occasions at Toronto and elsewhere after that period. . . . I am very sorry to say that the same reason which impeded his management of the elections was operating during the whole of the days the Parliament remained in Session, and we never had the full advantage either of his abilities and judgment or of his nerve and courage. A night of excess always leaves a morning of nervous incapacity and we were subjected to this pain amongst others."

While Alexander Campbell's portrait was certainly correct, it should be noted that Macdonald had incredible powers of recuperation. On the morning of Monday, November 3, 1873, towards the end of the long debate on the Pacific Scandal, Macdonald showed up in the House looking haggard and behaving like a man whose mind was befuddled with drink. By the evening, however, a miraculous change had taken place. It was time for him to speak and he was infused with energy and clarity. The House was packed, the atmosphere was electric. Lady Macdonald was in the gallery. So was Lady Dufferin, who listened to him with care and interest and reported everything to her absent husband (who, as Governor-General, could not attend the House of Commons).

Macdonald spoke for nearly five hours. With his eloquence and sincerity he completely won back the respect of his

listeners. "We have faithfully done our duty," he concluded.
"We have had party strife setting province against province. . . . I have been the victim of that conduct to a great
extent; but I have fought the battle of Confederation, the
battle of Union, the battle of the Dominion of Canada. I
throw myself upon this House; I throw myself upon this
country; I throw myself upon posterity; and I believe, and I
know, that, notwithstanding the many failings in my life, I
shall have the voice of this country, and this House, rallying
round me. And, sir, if I am mistaken in that, I can confi-
dently appeal to a higher court—to the court of my own
conscience, and to the court of posterity. I leave it to this
House with every confidence. I am equal to either fortune. I
can see past the decision of this House, either for or against
me; but whether it be for or against me, I know—and it is no
vain boast for me to say so, for even my enemies will admit
that I am no boaster—that there does not exist in this
country a man who has given more of his time, more of his
heart, more of his wealth, or more of his intellect and power,
such as they may be, for the good of this Dominion of
Canada."

His speech was regarded as a personal triumph and was
praised by all. It cemented his hold over those Conservatives
who were still loyal to him and who came to be called the
"Old Guard", but it was not enough to save the government.
The public's confidence in the régime was gone, and as public
confidence vanished, Macdonald's parliamentary majority
dwindled. As Alexander Campbell explained, "from day to
day we had the painful experience . . . of hearing each morning that some supporter had dropped away and was about to
vote against us." Sir John knew that his government was
finished. Having no desire to face the humiliation of defeat in

the House of Commons, Macdonald resigned as Prime Minister on November 5, 1873.

He broke the news to Agnes in characteristic fashion. After submitting his resignation to Lord Dufferin, he returned home. "Well, that's got along with," he said quietly. "What do you mean?" replied Agnes. "Why," answered Canada's first Prime Minister, "the Government has resigned." As he put on his dressing-gown and made himself comfortable with a couple of books, he added: "It's a relief to be out of it."

The Pacific Scandal destroyed Macdonald's first government. Would it also destroy his career?

6

Interregnum

Observers of Canadian politics have often argued that federal governments fall because of their own blunders, not because of the brilliance or popularity of their opponents. That is, opposition parties win by default. Whatever the merits of this argument over the long run, it is an accurate description of what happened in 1873. The first Macdonald government fell because of corruption: after six exciting years it blundered into extinction.

Macdonald had been disgraced. He had no choice but to submit his resignation as party leader to the caucus of Conservative M.P.s and Senators. He did so on November 6, 1873, the day after his government fell. But loyalty carried the day for him and he was unanimously reaffirmed as party chief.

It was a greatly weakened party that Macdonald now led. This was revealed by the snap election called by Mackenzie for January 1874. The Conservatives won only seventy seats, half as many as the Liberals. Macdonald won Kingston, but was unseated when it was proven that citizens had been bribed to vote for him. In the by-election that followed he won his seat, but by only seventeen votes. To most observers Macdonald was finished, a used-up and dishonoured man. The vote of confidence he had received from his party in

November 1873 was not really very meaningful. Most observers, and Macdonald himself, assumed that he would retain the leadership for only a brief period before making way for a younger man. At the same time the defeated and shaken Conservatives could not immediately reject their leader without admitting his guilt in the Pacific Scandal. This they were unwilling to do.

Dr Charles Tupper was widely regarded as the heir to Macdonald's mantle—in spite of his excessive fondness for women. Macdonald encouraged this expectation. To a Kingston audience he said: "I have long been anxious to retire from the position I have held, and I am sure you will say, from the acquaintance that you have formed tonight with my friend, the honourable Charles Tupper, that when I do retire, he is a man who will fill my place." But Tupper was not yet a national figure. Sir John was still the only Conservative with a national reputation and he remained the party's shrewdest politician. He could hold the leadership if that was his real ambition, and it was.

He was tough and flexible and did not seem to care about public opinion. He would let Mackenzie have his chance. Macdonald realized that the new Prime Minister would make blunders and that the Liberal Party would be difficult to lead. He also knew that strong criticism of the new government would be unpopular. When his colleagues criticized him for not attacking the Mackenzie régime with firm vigour, he answered simply: "Give the Grits rope enough and they will hang themselves." He bided his time and attended to personal affairs.

Leisure was pleasant after ten years in office. Once again Macdonald had time to think and read. Reading had always been an important part of Sir John's life. He devoured the novels of Charles Dickens, Anthony Trollope, and Benjamin Disraeli. The plays of Richard Sheridan attracted him, as did such serious works as Lord Mahon's *The History of England from the Peace of Utrecht to the Peace of Versailles* (in seven volumes) and Thomas Carlyle's *Life of Schiller*. His interest in literature was as extensive as his interest in people, and he enjoyed reading "yellowbacks, tales of the most blood-curdling horrors, of the most approved blood-and-thunder type". He did most of his reading in bed, both after retiring at night and before getting up in the morning. With his superb memory he could always illustrate a point or enliven a speech with a serious or humorous literary reference.

Macdonald had no private wealth. After 1867 he depended on his prime-ministerial salary of $5,000 a year. When it became apparent during his 1870 illness that he was bankrupt, a group of his friends collected a testimonial fund for him. During the serious phase of his illness, when he was expected to die, it was assumed that the fund would be for the benefit of his wife and invalid daughter. In 1871-2, $67,500 was raised under the leadership of Hewitt Bernard, Macdonald's brother-in-law, and three wealthy Torontonians: Senator G. W. Allan, Casimir Stanislaus Gzowski, and Senator David Macpherson. Macdonald recovered, of course, and the earnings of the fund—about $4,000 per year—were used to ease his financial worries. The Trust Deed explained why the money was raised: "Whereas certain persons being desirous of presenting the Honourable Sir John Alexander Macdonald with a substantial Testimonial of their admiration for him as a Statesman and of their esteem and regard for him personally have contributed in various amounts the sum of Sixty Seven thousand five hundred dollars . . ."

The income from the testimonial fund was a great boon to

Sir John, but when he lost his salary as Prime Minister in 1873, he could not live on $4,000. His first need was to provide a living for his wife and daughter. His law firm had moved from Kingston to Toronto in 1871. After his government fell in 1873 he rejoined his law practice in order to provide the income his family needed. For over a year he retained his Ottawa home while spending a great deal of time at his Toronto office. This was a grossly inconvenient arrangement, so in 1875 he rented a large house on Sherbourne Street and moved his family to Toronto.

The Macdonalds settled in quickly. Sir John was busy—as he was during most of his life. He devoted himself to the practice of law, but he was still Leader of the Opposition in the House of Commons. Politics were constantly on his mind, but for a while at least he was able to watch and wait for his chance to stage a political comeback.

The new Prime Minister, Alexander Mackenzie, was undistinguished. Like Macdonald, he was a Scot by birth. He too settled in Kingston but he left eastern Ontario to live in Sarnia. He was a stonemason and became a prosperous builder and contractor who was also active in the Liberal politics of Canada West. Mackenzie developed a bitter hatred for Tories. He was serious when he commented: "The heart of the average Tory is deceitful above all things and desperately wecked [sic]." He was elected to the Assembly in 1861 and to the Parliament of Canada in 1867. A dour little man with a grey beard, Mackenzie was sensible and honest but he lacked imagination and was never a strong leader. He could not match Macdonald's quickness or his gift for political manipulation. He was also unlucky, for he came to power at the wrong time. The Liberal Party lacked roots outside central Canada. Mackenzie's position as leader was therefore insecure and Canada's first Liberal cabinet was weak and unstable.

Two more important problems over which Mackenzie had no control further undermined the effectiveness of his government. The first was economic. Shortly after the Liberals took power, the world depression of the 1870s descended upon Canada. Most government income came from customs duties, which declined with reduced trade. As a result Mackenzie's government found it difficult to begin or continue costly programs. The second insoluble problem was the promised railroad to the Pacific. Most Liberals, including Mackenzie, opposed the line and were not anxious to build it; in fact they could not build it because government revenues were declining.

Mackenzie tried to substitute a new railroad policy, which would have meant building the railway in sections to allow more time for construction and to avoid the expensive work north of Lake Superior. The result was a wail of agony from British Columbia that quickly became a bitter quarrel between the federal government and the Pacific province. British Columbia insisted that Canada live up to her promise to build a transcontinental railroad connecting B.C. with the St Lawrence valley. Mackenzie and many of his supporters argued that the country could not afford to construct the railroad during a depression and at the expense of the eastern-Canadian taxpayer. To these men B.C. was not worth the trouble and expense—hence Edward Blake's description of the province as "that inhospitable country, that 'sea of mountains' ". British Columbia's government was so furious with Mackenzie's government that the province threatened to secede from confederation.

There was a difference of opinion within the Liberal Party

on the question of the transcontinental railroad. One group, led by Edward Blake, was opposed to rapid construction if it would mean increased taxation (which of course it would). They did not take B.C.'s complaints very seriously. "They won't secede," argued Blake, "they know better." Another group, however, believed that there had been a commitment and that an honest attempt must be made to live up to it. The quarrel dragged on for years. Prime Minister Mackenzie was never able to find a solution acceptable to both British Columbia and his own party.

Macdonald knew that Mackenzie's government was vulnerable. The depression produced gloom throughout the land; the Liberals looked inactive and indifferent. The quarrel with B.C. intensified, and was complemented by growing opposition to the Liberal Party in Quebec. When the public became restive, the Conservatives started to win by-elections. Conservative spirits rose and Macdonald realized that it was time to act.

A dynamic and popular policy was needed. Macdonald and Tupper found one in the famous National Policy, which came to be called the N.P. High tariffs would be introduced to protect native industry from foreign competition: by increasing the price of imports they would make it easier for Canadian manufacturers to compete with goods imported from Britain and the United States. Numerous manufacturing plants would then be established to serve the needs of the protected home market and especially of the expanding West. This policy of protection was economic nationalism, representing a desire to make Canada economically independent and to preserve it for Canadians. ("Canada for the Canadians" was Macdonald's slogan for it.) The completion of the CPR would bind together East and West: the new railroad

Making Sir John a Chief, Council House of the Six Nations Indians, near Brantford, Ont.

would enable the West to purchase goods manufactured in central Canada and would carry wheat from the Prairies to Atlantic ports. Finally, a vigorous immigration policy would provide settlers for the West, both to grow wheat and to buy the goods manufactured by the protected industries. The N.P. was a logical extension of confederation, which was partly the result of a desire for political independence, and started to take shape in Macdonald's mind during his first confederation government. He had in fact used the term "National Policy" as early as 1872.

High tariffs, the rapid construction of the CPR, heavy immigration—this was the N.P., and it was anathema to Liberals, who supported free trade and hated protective tariffs.

With their confidence restored, the Conservatives took the offensive. After 1876 the Liberals were given no peace. Macdonald planned to destroy the unimaginative government of Alexander Mackenzie and avenge his humiliating defeat of 1873-4. He presented his case in an unusual but highly effective manner. In 1876, 1877, and 1878, the Conservative Party staged a series of political picnics. These were arranged by local Conservative leaders, often at the farm of a supporter. Massive amounts of fine country food were prepared and barrels of whisky were collected. Hundreds of citizens piled into their carriages or wagons and drove in for the fun— whether they were Conservative, Liberal, or neutral. The picnics were family affairs. Children played; mothers served home-made food—hams, cold cuts, roast turkeys, bread, jams, preserves, cheese, cakes and candies; fathers talked and drank whisky, most of which was probably distilled on the farm.

Sir John Macdonald was the star of these occasions. Picnics were ideally suited to his style and talents. As he strode through the crowds he would address dozens of men and women by name. When the festivities were well under way Sir John would make one of his happy but partisan speeches. Crops were poor in the mid-1870s. Macdonald explained why: "It only goes to show that Providence is on our side . . . While we were in power, there were splendid crops, good prices, no weevil, and no potato-bugs. We are going to have a good crop now though a Grit government is in—but the reason is this: *the Grits are going out!*" "Be sure, my friends," he assured another group of delighted picnickers, "that the weevil will come again with the Grit." During these late years of Mackenzie's government, Macdonald was at his partisan best. He was obviously unfair in blaming the Liberals for bad crops, the weather, and pestiferous insects like weevils and potato-bugs—unfair but effective, for the crowds loved it. The depression annoyed everybody, and apparent government inactivity infuriated large sections of the public.

After flailing the government unmercifully, Macdonald would describe his National Policy and explain how it would solve Canada's problems. Bitter about the depression and the general economic hardship, people responded with enthusiasm. Sir John was not embarrassed by the fact that for years he had been lukewarm towards protection—it was too popular a policy to waste! "Protection", he explained with gay cynicism, "has done so much for me that I felt I must do something for protection." As the general election of 1878 approached, the tempo of Macdonald's campaign against the Liberal Party increased in intensity.

The quarrel between Macdonald and the Liberals was bitter, and the bitterness infected the last session of the Parliament elected in 1874. Donald A. Smith, member for Selkirk, Manitoba, had deserted Macdonald's government over the

Pacific Scandal and had helped to force Macdonald out of office. Macdonald refused to forgive and forget. In 1878, just before Parliament was dissolved, Sir John and Charles Tupper raked up the whole business and got into a violent argument with Smith over his desertion in 1873. The quarrel was a memorable example of parliamentary bitterness. At one point in a debate Macdonald screamed: "That fellow Smith is the biggest liar I ever met!" This was recorded in *Hansard.* The *Hansard* reporter, however, failed to note what followed immediately after. Macdonald, still furious, lunged at Smith shouting: "I can lick you quicker than Hell can scorch a feather!" Fortunately several of Macdonald's colleagues intervened to prevent violence.

The general election of 1878 was coloured by animosity and sometimes hatred. Even so, Sir John's success was complete. Liberal incompetence, Macdonald's restored popularity, and the N.P. carried the day for the Conservatives. The results of 1874 were reversed. Sir John returned to power with a sweeping majority and the strong support of his own province. His achievement represented the most brilliant political recovery in Canadian history. The Liberal Party was to wander in the wilderness of opposition for eighteen years.

7

A Last Burst of Creativity

Sir John A. Macdonald was back in the Prime Minister's office in the East Block of Canada's magnificent Parliament Buildings. He was delighted by his return to power, explaining to a group of supporters: "Trade revived, crops were abundant, and bank stocks once more became buoyant, owing to the confidence of the people of Canada in the new Administration. A citizen of Toronto assured me that his Conservative cow gave three quarts of milk more a day after the election than before; while a good Conservative lady-friend solemnly affirmed that her hens laid more eggs, larger eggs, fresher eggs and more to the dozen ever since the new Administration came in." S. L. Tilley reappeared in Ottawa as Minister of Finance, charged with introducing protective tariffs. Charles Tupper was given first Public Works, then the new ministry of Railways and Canals. His was to be the immense task of supervising the construction of the Canadian Pacific Railway. Macdonald himself, Minister of the Interior as well as Prime Minister, was responsible for Western settlement. Other carryovers from the first government were included in the new cabinet. Hector Langevin was now the most powerful Conservative from Quebec. Senator Alexander Campbell and John Henry Pope, the tough and almost illiterate politician from Quebec, were back. It was an able cabinet, but it was comprised mainly of men who had recovered from the disaster of 1873. Five years of opposition had produced few new leaders.

Macdonald was sixty-three in 1878, with only one passion left: to lead the government of Canada. This he did until his death thirteen years later. Luck can make or break politicians and luck favoured Macdonald in 1878, for just as he returned to power the depression lifted. It was to descend again, but for a few years Canada was spared serious economic hardship. Macdonald was determined to see the National Policy put into effect and this period of prosperity was essential to raise the necessary large sums of money through loans or taxes.

Edward Blake, premier of Ontario in 1871-2 and Mackenzie's successor as federal Liberal leader, proclaimed in 1873 that "It is impossible to foster a national spirit unless you have national interests to attend to." The National Policy was the Conservative answer. Charles Tupper had said as much in 1876: "I say what Canada wants is a national policy—a policy that shall be in the interest of Canada, apart from the principles of protection." The second Macdonald government, during its early years, had a plan for national consolidation and proceeded to carry it out.

Protection was the first part of the N.P. that was put into practice, not only because it was important but because it was easy to make law. No immediate expenditure of money was required, and higher tariffs could be introduced as part of the federal government's annual budget. For several years after 1878 Minister of Finance Tilley expanded and modified Canada's system of protective tariffs. Like the United States and Germany, Canada became a high-tariff nation. Macdonald gave his party one of its traditional and most popular policies.

Protection, of course, was opposed by some Canadians. Until he died Macdonald was locked in battle on the issue. To nineteenth-century Canadians this was no dry and boring subject. Supporters of the N.P. regarded protection as necessary to Canadian independence and growth. They tended to regard their opponents as slightly disloyal. Enemies of protection were usually free traders, men who believed that barriers (economic or political) would hinder the sale of goods between countries. Like their British allies they believed that much of the friction between countries was caused by economic insecurity and poverty. Free trade, they believed, would help to produce economic security and world-wide prosperity; it was in their minds the key to world peace and co-operation. Emotions ran high. Alexander Mackenzie wrote: "Protection is a monster when you come to look at it. It is the essence of injustice. It is the acme of human selfishness. It is one of the relics of barbarism." Most farmers disliked protection because they wanted to purchase manufactured goods as cheaply as possible. The Maritimes and the West resented protection because most of the new factories were in Ontario and Quebec. But central Canadians, business, and the railroads were assisted by protection, so that Macdonald's ties with businessmen, bankers, railroadmen, and the cities were strengthened. This annoyed the Liberals, who claimed that these relationships were corrupt. They argued that in return for tariff favours, businessmen donated funds to the Conservative Party. In a number of instances they were right.

While Tilley revised the tariff, Macdonald studied the transcontinental railroad. The situation was far from desperate. Mackenzie, with little money and less belief in an all-Canadian route, had plodded away on railroad construction.

His bequest to Macdonald was the completion of several hundred miles of line and most of the survey work. A good start had been made, and the survey material would save enormous amounts of time. B. C. was assured that the government intended to live up to its earlier promise, and Macdonald set to work to find a group of businessmen able to finance and build a transcontinental railroad.

Success came in 1880 when Macdonald found a business syndicate willing to tackle the job. It formed the Canadian Pacific Railway and brought into association some remarkable men. George Stephen, president of the Bank of Montreal, headed the group. Stephen was a financial wizard with a mind as steely as CPR track. He believed in the line, and was willing to take hazardous risks to see it completed. Stephen's most important partner was Donald A. Smith (later Lord Strathcona). Smith was a high official of the Hudson's Bay Company and a financier. In 1869-70 he had acted as Macdonald's agent in Red River, but because of his desertion over the Pacific Scandal, Macdonald found it difficult to co-operate with him in any way; he prized loyalty very highly. As a consequence Smith's connection with the syndicate remained a secret for some time. Sir John, of course, knew that Smith was a key backer of the CPR but could not bring himself to admit publicly that the hatchet had been buried. Stephen and Smith had many associates and subordinates, but their most famous were two Americans: William Van Horne and T. G. Shaughnessy. They supervised the actual work of construction, revealing themselves during the 1880s as great railroad builders.

No syndicate could build the CPR without public assistance; the task was too large, the risks too great. Macdonald negotiated with members of the CPR syndicate. The terms of the agreement between the government and the CPR were part of the railroad's charter approved by Parliament in 1881. The company was given the track already built or under contract (worth almost $38,000,000), 25 million acres of western land (substantially larger than Scotland), a cash subsidy of $25,000,000, and a railroad monopoly in western Canada for twenty years. It also received tax relief and numerous government favours. In return the company was to complete an adequately constructed railroad by May 1, 1891.

Completing the CPR was a colossal task. The Liberals, led by Edward Blake from 1880 to 1887, vehemently fought the charter. They had never supported an expensive railway linking Canada with British Columbia. This persistent opposition embarrassed the government, made it more difficult to finance the line, and assisted the business enemies of the CPR.

On several occasions during the construction period the company came to the end of its financial tether, a problem made more difficult by the return of the depression in the 1880s. These crises turned out to be political as well as financial because the company had to resort to the government for funds. Macdonald could not agree to additional aid without the approval of Parliament. Seeking such approval was politically risky because the high cost of the line irritated central Canadian and Maritime taxpayers, and of course the Liberals were quick to exploit the issue. However, each time the CPR got into serious financial trouble and asked for help the government, after protracted discussion, agreed to ask Parliament to advance the money. Without these loans the CPR would have gone bankrupt. In 1883 the Hon. J. H. Pope, Minister of Agriculture, commented to a group of CPR officials who had appealed to Sir John for a loan: "Well boys, he'll do it. Stay over till tomorrow. The day the Canadian

Pacific busts, the Conservative party busts the day after." Sir John could not permit the CPR to go under or the Conservative Party to "bust".

Enormous natural obstacles were added to financial and political difficulties. Construction through northern Ontario was a nightmare. Tracks and engines sank into the muskeg, while blackflies almost devoured the workers. The prairies proved to be less flat than had been realized, which increased costs and slowed progress. In British Columbia construction was slow, expensive, and dangerous, for the mountains required tunnels and the rivers bridges. Thousands of Chinese were brought to Canada to build the B.C. section of the line. Abused, exploited, overworked, persecuted, then forgotten, they contributed enormously to the building of the railroad and thereby to Canadian development.

The gigantic project was constructed simultaneously in three regions: northern Ontario, the Prairies, and British Columbia. Thousands of men were employed, millions of dollars spent. Stephen, Smith, Van Horne, Shaughnessy, and their political allies pressed on through every crisis with relentless determination and courage. To the amazement of most Canadians the line was completed on November 7, 1885—over five years early. Macdonald then went west for the first time. In the summer of 1886 he and his wife travelled via the Canadian Pacific Railway to the Pacific. For this historic trip the CPR provided them with a luxurious private car, the *Jamaica,* though they sometimes viewed the passing scenery from the cowcatcher, the buffer projected in front of the engine and over the track.

Sir John was finally seeing the country he had done so much to create. It was a triumphant journey. Enthusiasm was tremendous and at every stop the Macdonalds were fêted and

presented with addresses. Joseph Pope, Macdonald's secretary, described in his memoirs the Prime Minister's arrival in
Manitoba's young capital: "Sir John had quite a reception at
Winnipeg, where a large number of people assembled to
receive him. Among the crowd gathered round the car was an
enthusiastic young Tory who was cheering with all his might.
Upon Sir John's appearance the enthusiasm became tremendous. When the lull came, the young Tory, who evidently had
never seen Sir John before in his life, remarked in a low voice
to a friend standing by, 'Seedy-looking old beggar, isn't he?'
and then resumed his cheering with redoubled vigour, as
though determined that his private impressions should not be
allowed to interfere with his party loyalty."

While the Macdonalds were in Vancouver an incident occurred that illustrated one of Sir John's most valuable political talents: an unmatched ability to remember people. While
he was walking about the streets a man came up to him and
said: "Sir John, I suppose you don't remember me." "Oh
yes," replied the Prime Minister, "I met you at a picnic in
1856, and you may remember it was a rainy day." "Yes,"
replied the surprised and flattered man, "that was the very
occasion."

Macdonald's first glimpse of the Pacific was a moving
experience. "As I stood on the shore of the Pacific by the
side of that old man, with his grey hair blowing across his
forehead," Pope wrote, "I could not help feeling what an
exultant moment it must have been for him. Here was the
full realization of his political dream of years. His chief
opponent had left on record his belief that all the resources
of the British Empire could not build the road in ten years.
Here it was built, out of the resources of Canada, in less than
half that time. It was no paper road, this. He had travelled

*Sir John and Lady Macdonald on their CPR coach
at Port Arthur, Ont., 1886*

over it himself. With his own eyes he had witnessed the marvellous feat. Here was the car which had brought him from Ottawa. Here, too, lapping his feet were the waters of the Pacific Ocean. His dream had become an accomplished fact!"

If Macdonald's achievement had been limited to his part in creating the CPR, he would still be regarded as a great Canadian.

Protection encouraged the growth of industry; the railroad provided an all-Canadian route that linked the Atlantic with the Pacific. These achievements were significant, but they were not enough. If Canada was to thrive as a transcontinental nation the West would have to be filled with people. This phase is usually regarded as the least successful aspect of the National Policy. While it is true that development was slow in the Northwest Territories, this criticism is unfair if applied to Manitoba, which underwent rapid and sustained growth during the period of Macdonald's ascendancy and experienced a boom in the 1880s. Land values increased and settlers, many from Ontario, flooded into Manitoba. Thousands of acres were put under the plough and wheat was finally produced for foreign export.

Two additional actions of Macdonald's second government enlarged and strengthened the young Dominion. In 1880 Canada took over from Britain the Arctic archipelago—the vast territory north of the lands granted to the Hudson's Bay Company in 1670. These lands became part of the Northwest Territories, which in the nineteenth century included the present provinces of Saskatchewan and Alberta. With the exception of Newfoundland, which stayed out of confederation until 1949, this transfer brought Canada to her present size.

Also in 1880 Canada appointed her first diplomatic representative abroad when Sir Alexander Galt became High Commissioner in London. This simplified Anglo-Canadian contacts and strengthened Canada's alliance with Britain. Macdonald believed strongly in close Anglo-Canadian co-operation as a counterweight to American power. His role in the development of Canadian external policy should be noted, for it is often forgotten that he was as devoted to Canadian independence as were Sir Wilfrid Laurier and Sir Robert Borden. In 1871, when Sir John helped to negotiate the Treaty of Washington, he strove to defend Canadian claims. In 1880 he appointed our first diplomatic representative to Britain, and for the rest of his life kept strong and able Canadian High Commissioners in London. (Sir Charles Tupper, for example, succeeded Galt.)

While Macdonald believed in a strong Anglo-Canadian alliance, he was not slavishly devoted to British interests: he could not therefore support a foreign policy common to the whole Empire unless it was also beneficial to Canada. This point was dramatically illustrated in 1885 when many Canadians wished to send troops to aid in the relief of Khartoum, which General Gordon (a popular Englishman) was defending against Sudanese tribesmen. Sir John's view was straightforward: Canadians had no interest at stake in North Africa. "Our men and money", declared Macdonald, "would be sacrificed to get Gladstone [Britain's Prime Minister] and Co. out of the hole they have plunged themselves into by their own imbecility." British involvement there was British business and Britain should solve her own problems with her own men and treasure. Successors like Laurier and Borden faced different problems, but they followed Macdonald's policy of building a strong and independent Canada.

Not all of Sir John's decisions during this period had positive and pleasant consequences. Some were ugly. Sir John was determined to maintain the support of his home province and never again to lose a federal election. He developed an obsession on the former point, perhaps because for years he led a minority group from Canada West. According to the British North America Act, representation by population in Parliament was to be maintained by a redistribution of federal constituencies after each decennial census. While rep-by-pop meant that each province was to have the number of M.P.s warranted by its population, no constitutional provision required that seats within a single province contain an equal number of electors. Consequently constituencies could and did vary tremendously in the size of their voting population. A redistribution that provides an advantage for one party over another is called a gerrymander. Until recently Canadian redistributions were always conducted by committees of the House of Commons, were almost always designed to assist the governing party, and were normally attacked by the Opposition.

The 1881 census returns necessitated a redistribution of Ontario's seats: the province was entitled to an additional four M.P.s. This gave Macdonald an excuse to distribute townships in such a way as to maximize Conservative strength and minimize Liberal strength. At the same time the Liberals were "hived"—that is, as many strong Liberal townships as possible were packed into a small number of seats. This would produce massive Liberal majorities in a few areas, but thousands of Liberal votes would be wasted. Macdonald was delighted; the Liberals roared their impotent fury. It is characteristic of Macdonald's approach to politics that he found humour in this situation. To a group of Conservative supporters he declared: "The Grits complain that they are hived all together. It seems they do not like the association—they do not like each other's company. They like to associate with Conservative gentlemen such as you. Your being with them rather gives tone to their society." The voters were apparently unimpressed by the controversy, for the Great Gerrymander had little obvious impact on the 1882 election. The Conservatives, with abundant funds from protected manufacturers and friendly railroaders, won an easy victory.

Another unhappy characteristic of the period was increasingly vociferous provincial and regional discontent. When Macdonald surveyed the Canadian scene at the outset of 1885 it must have seemed that the very existence of confederation was threatened. In Nova Scotia economic discontent was turned into another anti-confederation movement. It was an accident that Nova Scotia's decline became acute during the years following confederation, but the coincidence was sufficient. Many Nova Scotians blamed confederation for their province's ills, and local politicians exploited that feeling. Men like W. S. Fielding directed the anti-confederation movement, which culminated in 1886 with passage through Nova Scotia's legislature of a series of resolutions demanding Nova Scotia's release from the union. Fielding won a provincial election on the issue later in 1886, but the resolutions were never implemented.

In Ontario, Macdonald's former law student, Oliver Mowat, had been the Liberal premier since 1872. Although a Father of Confederation, he was a bitter foe of a strongly centralized federation. Mowat became one of Macdonald's most persistent enemies and Canada's greatest exponent of provincial rights. During the 1880s he fought Sir John on a whole series of issues, and was largely successful in bringing

Old Guard Dinner, House of Commons, 4 May 1882. "Sir Leonard [Tilley] led the House to-night while Sir John Macdonald, Sir Charles Tupper, Messrs Bowell and Mousseau, Sir Hector Langevin, and forty members of the Opposition in the last Parliament [1874-8] who hold seats in this, and dined in the Commons restaurant."—The Globe. The ladies joined the men for the toasts and then withdrew, and the party continued "fast and furious". This composite photograph, by William James Topley, was made by designing and painting the background and photographing each person in a predetermined pose after the event; a print of each photograph was cut out and pasted onto the background. The whole composite was then photographed and prints were sold to the public.

about a more even balance between the federal and provincial governments. Sir John was able to humiliate the federal Liberals over and over again, but in men like Mowat he met effective opposition that checked his plan to create a Canada dominated by the federal administration: the provinces too were to have a say in Canadian development.

Even little Manitoba had complaints. She felt that her subsidies were too small and her freight rates too high. From 1878 to 1887 Manitoba's premier was a Conservative, "Honest" John Norquay. For several years Premier Norquay supported Macdonald's railroad policy in exchange for financial considerations for Manitoba. But the clamour within the province grew. Manitobans wanted both larger subsidies and more than one railroad so that freight rates would be competitive and therefore (hopefully) lower. Norquay took too long to break his politically hazardous allegiance with the Old Chieftain, and the result was the fall of the Norquay régime. Manitoba was not powerful enough to be a real danger to confederation, but she became a constant irritation.

The most serious threat came from the Northwest Territories. After 1870 Manitoba became more and more a British province, dominated by settlers from Ontario. Riel pointed out in 1869 that in the event of "a large immigration" the Métis "would probably be crowded out of a country which they claimed as their own." He was a true prophet, for within a few years the exodus from Manitoba began. Hundreds of Métis families left for the Northwest Territories, where they settled the North Saskatchewan River area around Batoche. For a while they pursued their traditional way of life, but the buffalo died out and white settlers pushed into the far West. Once again they felt neglected and pressed. Their modest demands were summarized by one of their spiritual advisers,

Father Alexis André: "They demanded patents for their land, demanded frontage on the river, and the abolition of the taxes on wood, and the rights for those who did not have scrip* in Manitoba." Petitions were sent to Ottawa, but no useful answers were received.

In their bitterness and frustration the Métis sent a delegation to the self-exiled Louis Riel, asking him to return to Canada to lead his people. Riel agreed. With his family he travelled north from the United States in July 1884 to resume his role as Métis chieftain. Within a short time he headed a broadly based protest movement. White farmers were discontented because of the lack of both responsible government in the Northwest Territories and representation in Ottawa. They felt that the CPR should run westward through the northern park belt, not through the southern part of the district. Like Manitobans, they wanted cheap freight rates, subsidies, and rapid economic development. The Plains Indians—set aside on reservations that were much hated by a people who were once free and remained proud— were without buffalo. Many were desperate for want of food and starvation was not unknown. Indians, white settlers, Métis—all were discontented. Initially all looked with favour upon the leadership of Riel.

As in 1869, Macdonald refused to take the West seriously. His view was that a handful of agitators could not threaten Canada. This error resulted in tragedy, and in 1884-5 there was no doubt about who was responsible for maintaining order in the West. From 1878 to 1883 Macdonald himself was Minister of the Interior, personally responsible for supervising the administration of the Northwest Territories. Often

* A certificate entitling the holder to a specified number of acres of government-owned land.

problems were put off, particularly as he began to grow old. He was soon to learn that the problems of the Northwest Territories had been ignored for too long. Sir John was not called "Old Tomorrow"* for nothing.

If in early 1885 Sir John reflected on the accomplishments of his government since 1878, he had reason to be proud. Canada had become a high-tariff nation. The CPR had made magnificent progress. While development in the Northwest Territories lagged, Manitoba boomed ahead. New territories had been acquired and the fabric of confederation strengthened. Canada had established diplomatic representation abroad. The Conservatives won the election of 1882 and had a solid majority in the House of Commons.

Well and good—but the danger flags were up. The depression had again descended, and anti-federal agitations were gaining strength in Nova Scotia, Ontario, Manitoba, and the Northwest Territories. Tough problems were emerging just when the government was losing its ability to cope with difficulties. The Prime Minister and his cabinet were aging. Macdonald was seventy and often ill. Alexander Campbell was tired and left the government in 1887 to become Lieutenant-Governor of Ontario. Tupper preferred London to Ottawa, while Tilley resumed his post as Lieutenant-Governor of New Brunswick in 1885. Hector Langevin was embroiled in political battles in Quebec, and allowed himself to sink into a morass of corruption.

---

* It is perhaps significant that during Macdonald's lifetime many believed that his nickname "Old Tomorrow" was given him by a western Indian chief—either Poundmaker or Crowfoot. In Blackfoot the name is Ap-e-nag-wis. Indian chiefs had good reason to resent Macdonald's habit of putting problems off until tomorrow—over and over again! Macdonald knew about his nickname. When it was rumoured that he was to be elevated to a British peerage, he was asked what title he would take. With a perfectly straight face he replied: "Lord Tomorrow."

New blood was needed but was hard to find. John Thompson, a future Prime Minister, became Minister of Justice in September 1885. He was a brilliant man who strengthened the government. George Foster joined the cabinet in December 1885; he later became a competent Minister of Finance but was never a major leader. J. A. Chapleau, a former premier of Quebec, entered the government in 1882. He was also brilliant, but because of Macdonald's dislike and Conservative in-fighting he was not able to bring his full ability to the support of the government.

The simple truth was that the cabinet was declining and losing the flexibility and creativity necessary to the solution of new and difficult problems. Everything depended upon Macdonald. Lord Carnarvon, a leading British statesman, explained the situation when he visited Canada in 1883. Sir John, he explained, "stands like Saul, head and shoulders above all his contemporaries and colleagues, and wherever he might be he would have made his mark. His conversation has all the ripened wisdom and perhaps statecraft of an experienced statesman, and his knowledge of affairs in England and of parties there was remarkable. He did not seem very strong physically, and said that he felt weary at times of the work, but that his colleagues held him to it, and that several of them said they would not stay if he went."

8

Final Phase

Riel's western agitation became more intense. Late in 1884 he dispatched to Ottawa a petition demanding patents for Metis land, river frontage for his people's farms, tax relief, land scrip for those who had received none in Manitoba, better treatment for the Indians, freer trade, the secret ballot, and the construction of a railroad to Hudson Bay. Riel also advanced some personal claims. In February 1885 Macdonald's government responded with the promise that it would appoint a commission, conduct a census, and consider all Métis claims. To the Métis this answer meant more federal delay and thus spelled defeat. Their constitutional agitation had failed.

Rebellion followed. At Batoche in March 1885 Riel formed a provisional government called the Exovedate ("of the flock"). He was attempting to repeat his success of 1869-70, but radically different circumstances made repetition impossible. In 1885 nobody challenged Canadian ownership of the Northwest; there was no question of U.S. intervention; the almost completed CPR could prove its value by rushing troops west to assist the Mounted Police already on the spot.

The tragedy of the second Riel rebellion—or the North West Rebellion, as it is more properly called—was increased by the madness of its leader. Louis Riel behaved in irrational ways, and a recent study by a team of psychiatrists concludes that he was mentally ill. On one occasion he exclaimed: "You don't know what we are after—it is blood! blood! We want blood! It is a war of extermination." Riel believed himself a prophet, declaring at his trial: "I am the prophet of the new world." During the rising he did indeed behave more like a prophet than a political leader. Consequently the Exovedate concerned itself with theology at the expense of war. Bishop Bourget of Montreal was made Pope and the days of the week were given new names! This was the kind of leadership given to a handful of poor and badly armed Métis, who lost their white supporters when rebellion began. Indian allies were of no great military value, although they terrified the white communities. The Métis were on their own.

The rebels won some early victories. Under Gabriel Dumont they defeated a troop of Mounted Police at Duck Lake (Saskatchewan). The garrison at Fort Carlton, on the North Saskatchewan River, was then evacuated. At about this point some Indian bands rose, pillaged a few settlements, and at Frog Lake murdered several whites, including two priests.

Rebellion could not go unpunished. Unable to meet the legitimate demands of discontented westerners, Macdonald nonetheless could respond decisively to treason that challenged the state. A three-pronged assault was organized.

General Frederick Middleton, commanding the Canadian militia, led the most important expedition. He marched towards Riel's headquarters at Batoche. Major-General T.B. Strange, a veteran of the British Army, marched from Calgary to Edmonton, then east. His task was to pacify the Indians along the North Saskatchewan River. The third force, under Colonel William Otter, was also concerned with the military threat posed by rebellious Indians. Otter's men marched north from Swift Current to the relief of Battleford. Each expedition used the main line of the CPR as its base, proving the national importance of that great railroad.

The rebellion was quickly suppressed. After a check at Fish Creek, Middleton reached Batoche where a battle raged for four days. On May 9, 1885 the Métis were defeated. This time Riel did not escape and on May 15 he surrendered to Middleton. Riel was taken to Regina where he was tried for treason from July 28 to August 1. He was convicted and sentenced to die. After three reprieves he was finally hanged at Regina on November 16, 1885.

Macdonald was severely and justly criticized for allowing the situation in western Canada to deteriorate to rebellion. Métis demands in fact were not excessive and most were met once violence erupted. But the argument over the causes of the rising was superseded by Riel's execution, which provoked one of Canada's stormiest crises. Virtually all French Canadians, including Macdonald's cabinet colleagues, were opposed to the execution. Like the Liberals they believed that Riel was a madman who should be locked up. Most English Canadians, especially Ontario Protestants, wanted Riel hanged. To them he was twice a rebel and responsible for many deaths. Sir John was caught in this crossfire and after much thought and discussion agreed to the hanging. His motives have been questioned and attacked. To many critics his decision was another example of political opportunism. According to this school of thought Macdonald gave in to Ontario opinion because that province had more seats than Quebec: it was politically useful to execute Riel.

Such an explanation is excessively harsh. One must remember that Macdonald's whole career was based on a successful

A RIEL UGLY POSITION.

alliance with French-Canadian leaders and parties. He sympathized with French Canada and on more than one occasion
risked his position in Ontario to defend policies popular in
Quebec. It is nonetheless true that Sir John was always
sensitive to political realities. He was doubtless influenced by
deteriorating Conservative influence in Quebec. Langevin was
losing his grip and Chapleau was not accepted by all French-
Canadian Conservatives as their federal spokesman. This
made it difficult for the Quebec wing of the Conservative
Party to bring its full political weight to bear on the Riel
problem. At the same time Macdonald was anxious to hold
his Ontario majority. He himself was Ontario's federal leader
and he felt pressure keenly from that province. For many
years Riel had been a thorn in Macdonald's side, a nuisance
who refused to go away. Execution would permanently solve
a persistent and annoying problem.

But the most important explanation of Macdonald's decision to execute Riel probably lies in his approach to the
administration of justice. Like Alexander Campbell, who was
Minister of Justice until September 24, 1885, the Prime
Minister had a narrow view of the law. Riel was a traitor.
After his first offence he was pardoned. Now he must pay the
full penalty and die. French Canada might accept Riel's death
after the fact. J.A. Chapleau, who almost resigned from the
cabinet to lead a Quebec agitation against Ottawa, changed
his mind after looking over the brink, explaining to Macdonald: "I prefer the risk of personal loss to the national danger
imminent, with the perspective of a struggle in the field of
race and religious prejudices. We will have to fight, perhaps to
fall. Well I prefer, after all, to fight and to fall in the old ship
and for the old flag." Quebec, reasoned Macdonald, was
loyal. It would swallow the execution and stand by the

Conservative Party, as it always had.

Since mid-century the Roman Catholic Church in Quebec had been in turmoil. A kind of war raged between liberal and conservative Catholics. The fight was both political and theological. Most liberal Catholics supported the *Rouge* or Liberal Party. Their Catholic opponents were divided into two groups: moderate Conservatives, who accepted the supremacy of the state over the church, and ultra-Conservatives, who believed that the church was supreme in all situations involving morals (the line dividing moral and political questions was to be drawn by the church). The latter group was also very nationalistic. Its members were called ultramontanists and their religious leader was Ignace Bourget, Bishop of Montreal. In 1871 a group of Bourget's political followers published a document advocating ultramontanist policies for Quebec. This "Catholic Program" was highly publicized, and its supporters were called programists or Castors,* who came to represent the ultra-Conservative wing of the Conservative Party in Quebec. The result was a great conflict between Castors on the one hand and Liberals and moderate Conservatives on the other, because at stake were such fundamental issues as the role of the state in modern society and the place of French-Canadian culture within Canadian federalism.

During the 1870s and 1880s this strife threatened the very existence of the Conservative Party. Open division could make possible a Liberal victory in Quebec. For years a split was avoided, but as a consequence no single man could represent all Quebec Conservatives. After 1878 this factionalism became more acute. Langevin tended to sympathize with the Castors. Chapleau hated these "water skunks", as he

---

* A nickname given to them when they founded a newspaper, *L'Etendard,* the emblem of which was a beaver (*castor*).

called them on one occasion, with boundless violence: "they have only one trait in resemblance to the true beaver. They do their work with mud; they destroy the sluices of good mills to make their dens; and are useful only when their hides are sold."

Within Quebec a wave of indignation greeted Riel's hanging. The provincial Conservative Party was in power. Guided by Chapleau it refused to declare war on Ottawa. That left an opening for the Liberals, led by the ultra-nationalist Honoré Mercier. The provincial Conservative government was ridiculed for not assaulting the federal régime. As a consequence many ultra-Conservatives deserted their party and supported Mercier. Early in 1887 he formed a new provincial government, with the help of some ultra-Conservatives or Castors. The Conservative Party was publicly split and, like Humpty-Dumpty, was never properly put back together. Co-operation between moderate Conservatives and Castors was now impossible. They hated each other even more than they disliked Liberals. Ultimately the Castors came out on top within the Quebec wing of the federal Conservative Party and Chapleau's followers joined Laurier. This was a long process, but it accounts for a Liberal sweep of Quebec in 1896. Riel's execution set off a chain reaction. The Métis chieftain had the last laugh.

By 1885 both Sir John's régime and his career were in their final phase. His 1878 program was law and no new policies were forthcoming. The government had lost control. Instead of moulding and guiding Canadian destiny, it reacted to events and conditions. Often it reacted wrongly. Macdonald once said: "Anybody may support me when I am right. What I want is a man that will support me when I am wrong." After 1885 he had need of such men. The ministry was chiefly motivated by a desire to survive. Canada seemed to be disintegrating. The Northwest had been shaken by rebellion and controversy continued to rage around that event. The return of the depression produced renewed assaults on the National Policy. Quebec Conservatives fought each other. The premiers of Ontario, Quebec, Manitoba, and Nova Scotia, all dedicated to increasing provincial power, became more vicious in their assaults on federal authority. To many the CPR was an unnecessary and expensive luxury.

1887 was election year. It seemed clear that the Liberals would win this time, but to the amazement of many Sir John led his party to another victory. "An election is like a horserace," Macdonald once observed, "in that you can tell more about it the next day."

The Liberals, however, made substantial gains in Quebec, and the popular vote was close—51% for the Conservatives, 49% for the Liberals.

Sir John, at the age of seventy-two, was given another majority, his government another lease on life. Edward Blake, the Liberal leader, was simply not up to Macdonald's standard. While his Liberal colleagues loved him, the people were not attracted by what J.C. Dent described as "a manner as devoid of warmth as is a flake of December snow".

Macdonald's magnetism still remained the Conservative Party's greatest asset. Thousands of Canadians worshipped the old leader. One of his most devoted followers was Mrs Grimason, whose Kingston tavern was for years Macdonald's local election headquarters. She was thrilled when John A. invited her to visit Ottawa. While in the Parliament Buildings they encountered William Mulock, a distinguished Toronto Liberal. Macdonald introduced Mulock to Mrs Grimason, who immediately lectured him on his political sins. After

"Earnscliffe", a Macdonald home in Ottawa

warming up she startled the dignified gentlemen with the remark: "I hate them damn Grits!" Patrick Buckley, a cab driver, was another lifelong follower. For thirty-eight years he saw to it that Macdonald was driven to his proper destination. His loyalty never faltered and when Macdonald was out of power from 1873 to 1878, Buckley often refused to accept payment for his services. Macdonald even accepted advice from his humble friend. Buckley loved to recount one incident. Macdonald was to meet some important people. As he picked him up, Buckley commented: "Sir John, why didn't you put on your grey suit? You look much better in it." "Is that so, Buckley?" said Macdonald, and he went back to change. He always had time for ordinary Canadians and never lost his ability to make new friends. His sense of humour also stayed with him. When he visited Prince Edward Island in 1890, for example, he was asked to sign the visitors' book in the legislative library. He listed his occupation as "cabinet-maker".

The defeat of 1887 rocked the Liberal Party. The leadership changed: Wilfrid Laurier replaced Blake. Sir Richard Cartwright, a Kingstonian who bitterly hated Macdonald, became Laurier's Ontario lieutenant. The Liberal leaders set about finding a policy that was distinct from the N.P. The lack of such a policy had put Blake at a serious disadvantage because he could not pose as a distinct alternative to Sir John.

Supporters of the National Policy sought both political and economic independence for Canada; they strove for union on east-west lines, for a Canada able to control and shape her own destiny. Because they were convinced that the N.P. had failed, Liberals could no longer accept this approach and their uncertainty became despair in the late 1880s.

Therefore, they reasoned, let us start again with a plan—for continental integration. Cartwright, a dedicated free trader, had the answer. He and Laurier led the Liberal Party to the policy of "Unrestricted Reciprocity". This involved freedom of trade between Canada and the United States, with each country continuing its own tariffs against all other countries. The result would be a continental economy, with the flow of goods directed north and south rather than east and west. Unrestricted Reciprocity represented a major break with Blake's position and a fundamental assault on the National Policy. No longer would the Liberals argue for a modified N.P.: they wanted it destroyed.

Laurier and Cartwright argued that the National Policy had already failed. New trade routes were therefore necessary and would be economically healthy. Liberals believed that farmers, fishermen, lumbermen, and consumers would benefit from a bigger market for their produce and lower prices for their purchases. At the same time discussion of trade policy, which was an important economic issue, might divert attention from the racial bitterness that was destroying Canada's soul.

Unrestricted Reciprocity meant more than a policy for prosperity, an attack on one of Macdonald's key programs, or a good election issue. Supporters of Unrestricted Reciprocity were influenced by the depression and the consequent economic crisis. Thousands of Canadians left the country to find employment in the United States. As the Toronto *Mail* commented in 1887: "There is scarcely a farmhouse in the older provinces where there is not one empty chair for the boy in the United States." Unemployment was high, but many protected industries made huge profits. The West and the Maritimes were convinced that they were being exploited by central Canada. For many the CPR, a key part of the N.P., was an oppressor because of its high freight rates. The concept of thriving east-west trade impressed critics as a pipedream. When added to provincial-rights agitations, the recent western rebellion, and an economic depression, these problems seemed grim indeed. Many Canadians lost faith in their country's ability to survive. Laurier expressed these doubts to Blake in 1891: "We have come to a period in the history of this young country where premature dissolution seems to be at hand. What will be the outcome? How long can the present fabric last? Can it last at all?"

Unrestricted Reciprocity was Sir John A. Macdonald's last great challenge. Conservatives had always advocated a reciprocity arrangement, provided it was consistent with Canadian policy and planning; in 1871 and again in 1887 his government negotiated unsuccessfully with the Americans to that end. But Unrestricted Reciprocity Macdonald would not and could not accept. He made his position clear: only a limited form of reciprocity was acceptable and desirable. In spite of all his opportunism and skill at political manoeuvre, Sir John was emotionally committed to the National Policy and to his concept of Canada.

The Liberal Party threw down the gauntlet after the 1887 election. Macdonald picked it up and resolved to fight. But by this time he was both sick and old. It was to be a struggle to the death.

Macdonald lived his last years against a grim, stark background. Everything was exploding. J. C. Rykert, Conservative M.P. for Lincoln, involved himself and his party in a nasty scandal over the fraudulent sale of federal timber lands; it was only an example of many such incidents that rocked the government. Conflict within the Quebec wing of the party

Lady Macdonald, 1885

Sir John A. Macdonald, 1888

intensified, and was complemented by division in Ontario. One of Macdonald's brightest followers, D'Alton McCarthy, emerged as a leader of those Ontarians who were prejudiced against French Canadians. In 1890 Manitoba's Liberal government started a long national struggle by abolishing the separate schools guaranteed in the Manitoba Act. All the while the Liberals assaulted the policies that were most important to Macdonald. As many of his colleagues were ineffectual or no longer dedicated to public life, the old man still carried much of the government's burden. John Thompson was a great help, but he was only one man.

Macdonald planned and waited. He appeared to be unusually reasonable because he was quiet, allowing those with extreme opinions to hold the stage. As a result the country reverberated with the arguments of annexationists and supporters of Unrestricted Reciprocity. Early in 1891 an election was called for March 5. Macdonald marshalled his strength. The CPR would use its money and vast influence to help Macdonald win, for great interests were at stake. Protected industries would contribute or face ruin in the event of a Liberal victory. Tupper returned from England to assist his chief.

It was a remarkable campaign. The Prime Minister was seventy-six and for some time had not been well. Nonetheless he led his party actively and brilliantly until he collapsed from exhaustion on February 25. Macdonald was still a tough man, however, and was soon well enough to return to work.

The theme of Macdonald's last campaign was loyalty. "As for myself," he declared in his last election manifesto, "my course is clear. A British subject I was born—a British subject I will die. With my utmost effort, with my latest breath, will I oppose the 'veiled treason' which attempts by sordid means and mercenary proffers to lure our people from their allegiance." The Conservative campaign slogan was "The old flag, the old man and the old policy".

Unrestricted Reciprocity, he claimed, was merely a prelude to annexation. The Liberals were pursuing policies that would lead to Canada's absorption by the United States. "They have as many aliases for their policy as a thief has excuses for his wrong-doing," Sir John trumpeted. "It has been commercial union, unrestricted reciprocity, and latterly tariff reform; but there is another name by which it must be known, and that is annexation—which is treason."

In February he was able to produce evidence to prove his point. Edward Farrer, a leading *Globe* editorial writer, had written a pamphlet listing several steps the American government might take to force Canada into union with the United States. The few copies printed were not to be publicly circulated, but the *Globe* was regarded as a Liberal journal and Farrer as a Liberal spokesman. The Conservatives obtained part of the pamphlet from a printer who stole it, probably for a price. This evidence enabled Macdonald to use the loyalty cry with great effectiveness. At a dramatic rally in Toronto the Tory chieftain exposed the Liberal Party to shame and ridicule: "I say that there is a deliberate conspiracy, in which some of the leaders of the Opposition are more or less compromised; I say that there is a deliberate conspiracy, by force, by fraud, or by both, to force Canada into the American union." Farrer's pamphlet, he continued, "points out every possible way in which Canada and its trade can be injured and its people impoverished, with the view of eventually bringing about annexation."

Macdonald turned the election into a test of basic loyalty. In spite of tremendous odds, for his government was hopelessly weak, he succeeded to the extent of winning a last majority. After the dust cleared the Conservatives had 122 seats to the Liberals' 91. The Liberals won a paper-thin majority in central Canada; the outlying areas carried the day for Macdonald. This prompted Sir Richard Cartwright's taste-less and famous comment that Macdonald's majority depen-ded on the "shreds and patches of confederation".

Macdonald's purpose was accomplished. He had beaten back the most powerful assault ever launched against the National Policy. The Liberal Party rethought its policy of Unrestricted Reciprocity and dropped it shortly after the election. (With only minor modifications Laurier and the Liberal Party later adopted the N.P.)

One aspect of the election gave Sir John great personal happiness. His son, Hugh John, now a successful lawyer, was elected to Parliament as Conservative M.P. for Winnipeg. Hugh John's introduction to the House of Commons was an emotional experience for the Macdonald family. Sir John and his son took the members' oath and "together fixed their autographs to the parchment, the son signing on the line below Sir John." Macdonald then entered the chamber of the House of Commons "arm in arm with his son", observed a newspaperman. "The old chief never looked better. He was dressed in a frock coat with light trousers, with the tradi-tional red neck-tie and a 'stovepipe' hat. His eye was clear, his step elastic, and everything betokened that he was in good condition for the hard work of the session."

Sir John's appearance was deceptive. After his collapse on February 25 he had been taken to Earnscliffe, his Ottawa home. Several weeks of rest restored his strength sufficiently to enable him to return to work, but he was weak and tired. In late May he suffered a stroke, which produced a deepening paralysis. For many days he lingered between life and death. Canadians knew that the end was near, and the country seemed to hold its breath while the government almost ceased to function. Political battle was postponed. Street cars near Earnscliffe stopped ringing their bells and on the Ottawa River steamers slowed their engines in order to give Sir John the quiet he needed. In spite of a "hemorrhage of the brain" Macdonald lingered. As always he responded to challenge with struggle and indomitable will. After losing the use of his voice he answered questions "by a gentle pressure of the hand . . ." Will was not enough, however, and he became weaker. Finally at 10:15 on Saturday evening, June 6, 1891, he died.

Canadians mourned the death of a man who had come to represent their country and its unity. Wilfrid Laurier spoke for many when he said in Parliament: "In fact the place of Sir John A. Macdonald in this country was so large and so absorbing that it is almost impossible to conceive that the politics of this country, the fate of this country, will continue without him. His loss overwhelms us."

Thousands of Canadians viewed Sir John lying in state in the Senate Chamber. He was then taken to St Alban's Church. After a service the funeral procession moved slowly through Ottawa to the railroad station, for Sir John was to be buried in Kingston. The weather dramatized the sadness of the day: "As the funeral car slowly passed the Parliament Buildings," wrote a prominent journalist, "the forked lightnings played above the tower, and, with the echoing crash of thunder, torrents of rain came down, drenching the processionists. It was the first thunder-storm of the season at the Capitol."

The black-draped funeral train was greeted by crowds at

The funeral of
Sir John A. Macdonald,
10 June 1891

every station between Ottawa and Kingston, where a crowd of 10,000 had gathered to mourn their old chieftain. Once again Sir John lay in state, this time in Kingston's City Hall. He was dressed in the uniform of an Imperial Privy Councillor and attended by an honour guard of Royal Military College cadets. Sir John was then buried near Isabella in the family plot in Cataraqui Cemetery, west of Kingston.

The Toronto *Empire* published a proper epitaph: "Canada was the object of his love and Canadian progress the product of his wisdom. To the people of Canada he gave, by and through the power of a popular party, the basis of its national structure and the bond of provincial unity."

But to thousands of Canadians the loss was more personal. At Sir John's funeral E. B. Biggar observed a grief-stricken old man. "Did you know Sir John?" Biggar asked. "Know him? Know him?" the man replied. "For thirty years I've known no other name."

Sources and Further Reading

Source material for the study of John A. Macdonald is both rich and extensive. The Public Archives of Canada holds the massive *Macdonald Papers*. This collection includes much of Macdonald's personal and public correspondence and is the most important single source for the study of his life. The PAC holds other important collections: the *Brown Papers*, the *Bowell Papers*, the *Galt Papers*, the *Thompson Papers*, and the *Laurier Papers*. This material is supplemented by several excellent collections in the Public Archives of Ontario: the *Cartwright Papers*, the *Campbell Papers*, and the *Blake Papers*. Queen's University holds the *Mackenzie Papers*. Newspapers are useful for the study of Macdonald and his age. Of special value are the following: Ottawa *Citizen*, Ottawa *Free Press*, Ottawa *Journal*, Toronto *Globe*, Toronto *Mail*, Belleville *Intelligencer*, Sarnia *Observer*, Kingston *British Whig*, and Kingston *News*. The House of Commons *Debates*, the Dominion of Canada *Sessional Papers*, the *Statutes of Canada*, and the reports of royal commissions of the period also provide useful material.

A vast amount of information concerning Macdonald and nineteenth-century Canada has been published in the form of articles and books. Only a brief introduction to this historical literature can be provided here. Paperback books are marked with an asterisk (*).

The most important study of Macdonald is Donald Creighton, *John A. Macdonald,* 2 vols (Toronto, 1952 and 1955). This great biography is essential for any serious study of Macdonald or his age. Joseph Pope, *Memoirs of the Right Honourable Sir John Alexander Macdonald,* 2 vols (London, 1894), written by his last private secretary, contains important documentary material. Pope later summarized his work in *The Day of Sir John Macdonald* (Toronto, 1922). E.B. Biggar, *Anecdotal Life of Sir John Macdonald* (Montreal, 1891) is a fascinating collection of stories about Sir John. One of Macdonald's cousins, J. Pennington Macpherson, wrote *Life of the Right Hon. Sir John A. Macdonald,* 2 vols (Saint John, 1891), which contains material on Macdonald's youth. Several other lives have been written. One of the best is a brief biography by W. Stewart Wallace, *Sir John Macdonald* (Toronto, 1924).

Articles provide studies of special aspects of Macdonald's career: Donald Creighton, "Sir John Macdonald and Canadian Historians", in Carl Berger (ed.), *Approaches to Canadian History: Canadian Historical Readings,* I (Toronto, 1967); Donald Creighton, "George Brown, Sir John Macdonald and the 'Workingmen' ", in the *Canadian Historical Review,* 1943; Donald Creighton, "John A. Macdonald, Confederation and the Canadian West", in Donald Swainson (ed.), *Historical Essays on the Prairie Provinces* (Toronto, 1970); P.B. Waite, "Sir John A. Macdonald: The Man", in Harvey L. Dyck and H. Peter Krosby (eds), *Empire and Nations* (Toronto, 1969); A.D. Lockhart, "The Contribution of Macdonald Conservatism to National Unity, 1854-78", in the Canadian Historical Association *Report,* 1939; P.B. Waite, "The

Political Ideas of John A. Macdonald", in Marcel Hamelin (ed.), * The Political Ideas of the Prime Ministers of Canada (Ottawa, 1969); and George F. G. Stanley, *The Man Who Made Canada, 1865-7 (New York, 1964).

Several volumes of Macdonald's letters have been published: Joseph Pope, Correspondence of Sir John Macdonald (Toronto, n.d.); J.K. Johnson, Affectionately Yours: The Letters of Sir John A. Macdonald and His Family (Toronto, 1969); and J.K. Johnson, The Papers of the Prime Ministers: Volume 1, The Letters of Sir John A. Macdonald, 1836-1857 (Ottawa, 1968). Other useful collections of documents are J.H. Stewart Reid, Kenneth McNaught, and Harry S. Crowe, A Source-Book of Canadian History (revised edition, Toronto, 1964); P.B. Waite, *Pre-Confederation (Scarborough, Ont., 1965); R.C. Brown and M.E. Prang, *Confederation to 1949 (Scarborough, Ont., 1966); and P.B. Waite, *The Confederation Debates in the Province of Canada (Carleton Library, Toronto, 1963).

Specialized studies help one to understand Macdonald's age. James A. Roy, Kingston: The King's Town (Toronto, 1952) and Margaret Angus, The Old Stones of Kingston: Its Buildings Before 1867 (Toronto, 1966) are good introductions to Macdonald's Kingston. P.B. Waite,*The Life and Times of Confederation: 1863-1867 (Toronto, 1964) and Donald Creighton, The Road to Confederation: The Emergence of Canada: 1863-1867 (Toronto, 1964) are the best accounts of the confederation movement. William Menzies Whitelaw, *The Maritimes and Canada before Confederation (Toronto, 1966) is a scholarly introduction to Canadian-Maritime relations. Gustavus Myers, History of Canadian Wealth (Chicago, 1914) includes excellent material on nineteenth-century political corruption. George F.G. Stanley, *The Birth *of Western Canada: A History of the Riel Rebellions* (Toronto, 1960) is the standard work on the rebellions of 1869-70 and 1885. G.P. de T. Glazebrook, *A History of Transportation in Canada,* 2 vols (Carleton Library, Toronto, 1964) is useful for the material it contains on the CPR and other nineteenth-century railroads. Pierre Berton, *The National Dream: The Great Railway, 1871-1881* (Toronto, 1970) contains a mass of fascinating material on the 1870s.

Macdonald's contemporaries should be studied if Macdonald and his age are to be understood fully. Books or articles have been written about several of his leading supporters: John Boyd, *Sir George Etienne Cartier, Bart.* (Toronto, 1917); Barbara Fraser, "The Political Career of Sir Hector Louis Langevin", in *Canadian Historical Review,* 1961; H. Blair Neatby and John T. Saywell, "Chapleau and the Conservative Party in Quebec", in *Canadian Historical Review,* 1956; O.D. Skelton, *Life and Times of Sir Alexander Tilloch Galt* (Carleton Library, Toronto, 1966); T.P. Slattery, *The Assassination of D'Arcy McGee* (Toronto, 1968); Donald Swainson, "Alexander Campbell: General Manager of the Conservative Party (Eastern Ontario Section)", in *Historic Kingston,* 1969; and Heather Gilbert, *Awakening Continent: The Life of Lord Mount Stephen,* Volume 1 (Aberdeen, 1965). For material on some leading opponents of Macdonald, see R. S. Longley, *Sir Francis Hincks* (Toronto, 1943); J.M.S. Careless, *Brown of the Globe,* 2 vols (Toronto, 1959 and 1963); D.C. Thomson, *Alexander Mackenzie: Clear Grit* (Toronto, 1960); George A. Rawlyk (ed.), *Joseph Howe: Opportunist? Man of Vision? Frustrated Politician?* (Toronto, 1967); H. Bowsfield, *Louis Riel: Rebel of the Western Frontier or Victim of Politics and Prejudice?* (Toronto, 1969); and O.D. Skelton, *Life and Letters of Sir Wilfrid*

Laurier, 2 vols (Carleton Library, Toronto, 1965).

For general historical background, see Kenneth McNaught, *The Pelican History of Canada* (Harmondsworth, 1969); Donald Creighton, *Canada's First Century, 1867-1967* (Toronto, 1970); J.M.S. Careless, *The Union of the Canadas, 1841-1857* (Toronto, 1967); W.L. Morton, *The Critical Years, 1857-1873* (Toronto, 1964); and Peter B. Waite, *Canada 1874-1896: Arduous Destiny* (Toronto, 1971). Arthur R.M. Lower, *Canadians in the Making* (Toronto, 1958) is a social history of Canada. Excellent general reference works are John C. Ricker and John T. Saywell, *How Are We Governed?* (Toronto and Vancouver, 1961); Norah Story, *The Oxford Companion to Canadian History and Literature* (Toronto, 1967); W. Stewart Wallace, *The Macmillan Dictionary of Canadian Biography* (third edition, Toronto, 1963); and *Encyclopedia Canadiana*, 10 vols.

Also useful in the preparation of this biography were Richard Cartwright, *Reminiscences* (Toronto, 1912); Joseph Pope, *Sir John A. Macdonald Vindicated: A Review of the Right Honourable Sir Richard Cartwright's Reminiscences* (Toronto, 1912); Charles Clarke, *Sixty Years in Upper Canada* (Toronto, 1908); George W. Ross, *Getting into Parliament and After* (Toronto, 1913); James Young, *Public Men and Public Life in Canada*, 2 vols (Toronto, 1912); Maurice Pope, *Public Servant* (Toronto, 1960); Sir Arthur Hardinge, *The Life of Henry Howard Molyneux Herbert, Fourth Earl of Carnarvon, 1831-1890*, 3 vols (Oxford, 1925); W.L. Morton, *Manitoba: A History* (second edition, Toronto, 1967); Margaret A. Ormsby, *British Columbia: A History* (Toronto, 1958); and Mason Wade, *The French Canadians, 1760-1967*, 2 vols (revised edition, Toronto, 1968).

Index